Programming
in
Fortran

CW00701788

OTHER BOOKS OF INTEREST

Programming in Fortran 77

by
Noel Kantaris

BERNARD BABANI (publishing) LTD
THE GRAMPIANS
SHEPHERDS BUSH ROAD
LONDON W6 7NF
ENGLAND

PLEASE NOTE

Although every care has been taken with the production of this book to ensure that any projects, designs, modifications and/or programs etc. contained herewith, operate in a correct and safe manner and also that any components specified are normally available in Great Britain, the Publishers and Author do not accept responsibility in any way for the failure, including fault in design, of any project, design, modification or program to work correctly or to cause damage to any other equipment that it may be connected to or used in conjunction with, or in respect of any other damage or injury that may be so caused, nor do the Publishers accept responsibility in any way for the failure to obtain specified components.

Notice is also given that if equipment that is still under warranty is modified in any way or used or connected with home-built equipment then that warranty may be void.

© 1988 BERNARD BABANI (publishing) LTD

First Published — August 1988

British Library Cataloguing in Publication Data:
  Kantaris, Noel
    Programming in Fortran 77.
    1. Computer systems. Programming languages:
    Fortran 77 language
    I. Title
    005.13'3

  ISBN 0 85934 195 X

Typeset direct from disk by Commercial Colour Press, London E7.
Printed and Bound in Great Britain by Cox & Wyman Ltd, Reading

PREFACE

Fortran is the most popular computer language (after BASIC) in use today. It is a powerful general-purpose programming language especially suited to complex scientific, mathematical, engineering, and financial algorithms. Thus, if you intend to write programs within these fields that need to be compact, fast in their execution, and yet transportable from one computer to another, then Fortran is the language you should be using.

Most people are familiar with BASIC, which unfortunately is not a very efficient computer language. A separate program called the BASIC interpreter, interprets each and every statement of a BASIC program every time it encounters it, into the machine code the particular computer can understand. Although lately BASIC compilers have been made available, they tend to be specific to a given BASIC dialect which itself is associated with a particular computer. In general, therefore, BASIC is slow in execution, and worse still, one computer's BASIC differs considerably from that of another.

Those who need to write fast execution programs, normally resort to writing in Assembler. However, programming in Assembler is a very tedious and slow process and has the added disadvantage of being different on different computers, thus making such programs almost impossible to transfer from one computer to another. Amongst the many languages that overcome the above limitations (Fortran, Pascal, C, etc), Fortran is by far the most popular language with the majority of today's programmers. It also has the additional advantage of being able to execute programs in both interactive and batch modes.

Fortran 77 is a structured language some features of which have been incorporated into some other popular languages running on IBM compatibles, such as BBC BASIC(86) and Turbo BASIC, particularly in the area of control of program flow. Programs can be written in modular form which when compiled provide the building blocks for larger and more complicated applications. A separate program, the Fortran compiler, is used to generate the machine specific code that will actually be executed by the particular computer. This means, of course, that instead of having to learn to program several computers in their own specific language such as Assembler or some dialect of BASIC, you only need to learn to program in Fortran.

This book is a guide to Fortran programming. Although similarities between Fortran commands and/or statements and those of other languages are occasionally highlighted in the text, the reader is not expected to have any familiarity with such languages. Fortran statements are introduced and explained with the help of simple programs. The user is encouraged to type these into the computer, save them, and keep improving them as more complex language statements and commands are encountered. Graded problems are set throughout the book, with full working solutions appearing at the back of the book. At the end of each Chapter additional graded exercises are presented, some with financial or scientific bend, so that users can choose their own level of problem difficulty on which to practice with some additional choice in the preference of the field of application.

Chapters 1-3 deal with the basic Fortran statements which control program flow and allow the user to manage with most aspects of the language, with the result that most general problems can be solved easily and effectively. Chapters 4-5 introduce the concepts of subprograms, strings and arrays which expand the programming capabilities of the user beyond the beginner's level. Chapter 6 deals entirely with numerical methods and should be of special interest to those in the fields of science and engineering, while Chapter 7 deals mainly with sorting techniques and disc file handling which should be of interest to all those who need to process large quantities of data.

Although the book is not limited to any specific Fortran 77 compiler, references are made to Microsoft's compiler which is discussed where appropriate to allow a user an understanding of the steps required to implement, compile, link and execute compiled code. The EDLIN line editor is discussed fully in Appendix A. Knowing how to use an editor to first produce and later correct Fortran source files is essential. Although this can be achieved with any word processing package which can produce an ASCII file, EDLIN is well suited for the particular job at hand.

CONTENTS

TRADEMARKS

MS-DOS and MS-Fortran are registered trademarks of Microsoft Corporation

IBM is a registered trademark of International Buiness Machines Corporation

BBCBASIC(86) is a trademark of M-TEC Computer Services

Turbo BASIC is a trademark of Borland International

1. LANGUAGE OVERVIEW

Fortran is a high level programming language which is easy to learn, but which remains extremely flexible. A program written in Fortran, called the source program, is compiled into machine code, called the object code, which is very compact and executes extremely fast. You can enter a new Fortran program in your computer with the use of either a full screen editor, or a line editor, such as EDLIN in MS-DOS, if you are using an IBM PC compatible. EDLIN is explained fully in Appendix A. Which editor you use depends largely on the type of computer being used. Indeed, you could use a word processor to enter a Fortran source file, provided it is of a type that creates an ASCII file.

In what follows, it is assumed that your editor is evoked by typing the appropriate command followed by the filename. For example, to create a Fortran source file called AVERAGE, using MS-DOS' line editor EDLIN, type

EDLIN AVERAGE.FOR (followed by pressing RETURN)

If the filename AVERAGE.FOR does not already exist on the disc, the editor will inform you of the fact that this is so and you can then start typing your new program, pressing the RETURN key at the end of each line. A program to calculate the average of three numbers will have to be entered as follows:

```
C CALCULATE AVERAGES
      READ *, A,B,C
      D=A+B+C
      AVER=D/3.0
      PRINT *, 'AVERAGE VALUE IS', AVER
      STOP
      END
```

The above program is presented to give an overview of what a Fortran source program is and how it is entered in the computer. All the Fortran statements contained therein will be discussed in detail in this and following pages. So there is no need to worry!

Note: Users of older installations should refer to the section entitled 'Device specification in READ and WRITE statements' as they might be required to use these in place of the READ and PRINT statements given above. Also, the filename extension is dependant on the compiler used.

Fortran statements

A Fortran source program consists of statements (one per line) and comment lines. Comment lines are identified by the letter C or an asterisk in the first column of the line, while all other statements begin on column 7 and should end on column 72. Columns 73 to 80 are used only for identifying the program and/or provide a statement sequence numbering system and are ignored by the compiler. Columns 1 to 5 are used for a statement label number, if a non-sequential transfer of program control is required, while column 6 is reserved for statement continuation identification.

To aid program readability the same program is shown below printed under a column identifier, as follows:

```
        1         2         3
12345678901234567890123456789 01  --- column position

C THIS IS THE SAME PROGRAM USED TO
C CALCULATE AVERAGES
      READ *, A,B,C
      D=A+B+C
      AVER=D/3.0
      PRINT *, 'AVERAGE VALUE IS', AVER
      STOP
      END
```

The above program consists of two comment lines and six statement lines. The numbers identifying the column position of these statements are not part of the source program and must not be typed into the editor. They have only been included in this text to show you the exact starting position of each statement.

The READ statement

The READ statement (first executable statement of the above program) provides one way of giving variables (see below for definition) a value. In the above example the READ statement is written with an asterisk after the word READ. This indicates that input will be provided from the standard input device which, when operating interactively, is the terminal keyboard.

2

The asterisk also implies that the values for the variables can be entered in any convenient free format — with or without a decimal point, or in exponential form. Fortran provides for a far greater flexibility in data input and output which indeed is one of the strengths of the language, but such enhancements will not be discussed at this point as they might confuse the newcomer to the language.

Once variables have values, they can be used in assignment statements and/or expressions in the rest of the program to perform desired calculations. A variable must have a value before it is used in an expression or in the right hand side of an assignment statement.

The PRINT statement

The PRINT statement (the fourth executable statement in our example program) allows the printing of the result of our calculation. This result is held in the variable named AVER. As with the READ statement, the asterisk following the word PRINT allows us to print the result of the calculation on the standard output device which, when operating interactively, is the terminal's video screen.

Again, the use of the asterisk allows us to delay discussion on formatting the printed output. However, the penalty is that we have to accept the default Fortran form of printing without any control on the number of digits printed out.

Following the asterisk there is information on what we intend to print out, enclosed in apostrophes (both being of the same form, namely the character '). The information was included in the program to make it easier for the user to identify the output. The variable AVER (which appears without apostrophes) follows a comma which separates items in a PRINT statement. Its use within the PRINT statement simply means that we wish to have its value printed out.

The STOP and END statements

It has been assumed throughout the foregoing discussion that program execution is sequential. The STOP statement halts execution of the program and can be placed in any part of the program, while the END statement signifies the physical end of our program to the compiler and as such must be the last statement encountered.

3

Device specification in READ and WRITE statements

A normal computer installation might have several different types of input/output (I/O) devices such as terminal keyboard, magnetic tape reader, monitor display, printer, plotter, etc., each one of which will have its designated number allowing the user the flexibility of entering input to the program via the READ statement and directing the output of a program to any of these devices via the WRITE statement. By convension, unit 5 is the standard input device and unit 6 is the standard output device (which you need to know if you ever have to examine older programs written in Fortran).

Thus the READ and PRINT statements of our example program are written as follows:

```
READ (5,*) A,B,C
```

and

```
WRITE (6,*) 'AVERAGE VALUE IS', AVER
```

Note the comma separating the device number and the asterisk (which allows free formatting) within the parenthesized section of both statements, and the omission of a comma between the closing parenthesis and the READ / WRITE list.

Variables, Constants and Expressions

Variables:
A variable is a quantity that is referred to by name, such as A, B, C, D and AVER in the above program. A variable can take on many values during program execution, but you must make sure that they are given an initial value, as Fortran does not do so automatically.

Constants:
A constant is a quantity that either appears as a number (3.0 in the third executable statement in the above program) or is referred to by name, but has only one value during program execution; that which was allocated to it by the user.

Expressions:
An expression, when referred to in this text, implies a constant, a variable or a combination of either or both, separated by arithmetic operators.

4

Of the five arithmetic operators, only the symbol for exponentiation (which is **) will be unfamiliar to the new comer. Thus, X**2 is interpreted as X^2. The reason why two asterisks are used to represent this operation is largely historical — in the early days of Fortran, keyboards were rather limited on the number of symbols available on them.

Variable names and constant names are formed by combining upper case letters with numbers (alphanumeric characters only), provided the first character is a letter and the length of the name does not exceed more than six characters.

There are a variety of types for both variables and constants. The most commonly used types are 'integer' and 'real' (otherwise referred to as floating point). An integer variable or constant can hold only integer quantities and is distinguished from a real variable or constant which holds real quantities containing fractional parts. The computer stores these two types differently and tends to calculate much faster when using integer-value variables or constants.

Examples of integer and real numbers are as follows:

-2
57   are integer numbers, while

1.0   are real or floating point numbers the last
$-.5$ two being in exponential form. Here the E is
$-.45E16$ interpreted as 'times ten to the power of'.

Less commonly used types of variables and constants are 'double precision' and 'complex', but will not be explored at this stage.

Implied integer or real variable types
The variable types can be implied integer or real by the first letter of the name describing a variable or constant. If the first letter is I, J, K, L, M or N (all the letters between and inclusive of the first two characters of the word INteger), the name implies that the element is integer; otherwise the name implies that the element is real.

If a real operand is assigned to an integer operand, the real is truncated to an integer, i.e. the statements

        I = 3.5   and
        K = 0.57

will cause Fortran to assign the integer values of 3 and 0 to the constants I and K, respectively. For this precise reason, mixing reals with integers, particularly while multiplying or dividing can have unexpected results! Thus, mixed mode arithmetic is best avoided.

Summary of some Fortran rules

* Variables and constant names must not be more than six characters long, can only contain letters and numbers and the first character must be a letter.

* Variable and constant names starting with I, J, K, L, M or N are assumed to hold only integer values. Remember the word INteger!

* Variable and constant names starting with all other letters are assumed to hold only real (floating point) values.

* Integer constants have no decimal point.

* Real constants must always have a decimal point.

* Mixed mode arithmetic is best avoided within an expression.

* The left hand side of an assignment statement must contain only one variable. This variable can be of different mode to the expression on the right hand side of the assignment statement.

* No more than one arithmetic operator can exist side by side in an expression. If the existence of two operators side by side is unavoidable, they must be separated by brackets. For example, A*(-B) is the correct expression for multiplying a positive variable A with a negative variable B.

* A number such as 20,000 can be expressed in exponential form as $.2 \times 10^5$. In Fortran this number is written as .2E5 and is a real constant. Similarly, a very small number such as .0000000005 should be expressed in the exponential form as .5E-9 — note that the exponent itself is an integer: it expresses only the number of zeros before or after the digit of interest.

* When raising a variable to a power, the power itself should be written in integer form whenever possible. For example, when squaring a number we should write A**2 which gives a more accurate result than A**2.0. Note that raising an integer to a real power, i.e. N**A, is not allowed as it is mixed mode. All other combinations, i.e. A**N, A**X and K**N are allowed.

Compiling and executing a program

The translation of a Fortran program (source file) to a machine specific code (object file) that will actually be executed by the particular computer is the task of the Fortran compiler. The compiled object file may or may not be executed immediately; it largely depends on the version of the compiler in your particular machine.

To illustrate the procedure of compiling and executing a Fortran program we shall use here the Microsoft Fortran Optimising Compiler (MS-Fortran, for short) in an MS-DOS operating environment. The exact steps taken in compiling the source file, linking the resulting object file to the appropriately selected library routines (supplied with the compiler), and then executing the resulting file, might vary slightly for different compilers, but the general philosophy remains the same.

It is assumed here that the Fortran compiler has been installed according to the instructions given in the installation manual of the package and that appropriate batch files have been written to allow access to the appropriate sub-directory in which the library routines are to be found.

For example, in the case of MS-Fortran, we assume that all files of the package have been copied to a sub-directory of the root directory which we shall call \MSFORT. When installing MS-Fortran with the SETUP command, three further sub-directories of the root directory are created by the program itself. These are:

\BIN	which contains compiler passes, linker, utilities, and error-message files,
\TMP	which contains temporary files, and
\LIB	which contains the library files.

To operate the system correctly, you must change the CONFIG.SYS file to declare at least 20 files open at the same time and also increase the number of buffers to 10. Use the EDLIN line editor to modify or add the command

```
FILES=20
BUFFERS=10
```

if necessary. Further, to allow easy access of the various library and utility files of the package, you need to modify and/or add to the PATH and SET commands to point to the correct sub-directories. All such changes could be incorporated into a batch file within the root directory which we shall call FORTRAN.BAT. Again we could use the EDLIN line editor to create the file with the following contents.

```
ECHO OFF
CLS
PATH=C:\;C:\DOS;C:\BIN
SET INCLUDE=C:\MSFORT\INCLUDE
SET TMP=C:\TMP
SET LIB=C:\LIB
CD\MSFORT
```

On executing this batch file, the directory is changed to \MSFORT and the environment is set correctly for the compilation of the source program and the linking of the resulting object file with the appropriate library routines to produce the executable file. However, before this can be achieved, we need to create the source program within this sub-directory, using the EDLIN line editor. For example, to create the AVERAGE.FOR file, simply type

```
EDLIN AVERAGE.FOR
```

and create it within the \MSFORT sub-directory.

Once the source program has been created we can compile it using a COMPILE.BAT file which must be found within the same sub-directory as the source program.

8

In the case of MS-Fortran, such a file will have the following contents.

```
ECHO OFF
CLS
FL /FPc %1.FOR
IF NOT ERRORLEVEL 1 LINK %1,,%1;
```

The precise form of the penultimate command in the above batch file depends on your hardware configuration. Here it is assumed that you have chosen the emulation maths package during SETUP. If you have a maths co-processor then the command takes the form

```
FL /FPc87 %1.FOR
```

Once this file has been created correctly, typing the command

```
COMPILE AVERAGE
```

causes the source file of the AVERAGE program to be compiled and linked to the appropriate library routines.

Note that in this instance, we have not bothered to separate the process of compilation from that of linking; a step that might be desirable under certain cirumstances, for example, when linking already compiled subroutines to a newly compiled program.

If compilation is successful, the system creates three files with the following extensions.

.OBJ	the object file,
.EXE	the executable file, and
.MAP	the map file containing all the linking addresses.

If there are any compilation errors, none of these files will be created. The compiler will simply inform you which line in your source file is in error. In such a case, use EDLIN to edit the original source file and re-compile. If there are no compilation or linking errors, execution of the program can be started by simply typing the name of the executable file, in this case,

```
AVERAGE
```

9

Note the cursor waiting for input. This will be the case with this particular program because we used the READ statement at the very beginning of the program and the computer is waiting for input.

Typing

2 3 5

the three numbers (separated by spaces or commas, if preferred) corresponding to variables A, B and C in the READ statement of the program, causes the computer to respond with

```
AVERAGE VALUE IS 3.333333
Stop - Program terminated.
```

To re-execute the program, we only need to re-type its name and supply different values to the program variables.

Finally, to provide a mechanism whereby we can quit the Fortran sub-directory and at the same time reset the system environment to its former settings, create a third batch file within the \MSFORT sub-directory with the following contents. Call this file QUIT.BAT.

```
ECHO OFF
CLS
CD\
SET INCLUDE=
SET TMP=
SET LIB=
PATH=C:\;C:\DOS
```

Note that the inclusion of the three SET commands, frees the DOS environment of the variables INCLUDE, TMP and LIB. As the DOS environment is limited in the amount of space allocated to it, it is prudent to eliminate these variables on quitting the Fortran compiler. Finally, the last entry in the file, can reset the system parameters to their original settings which existed prior to the use of the FORTRAN batch file, by setting the PATH to the original settings.

Thus, any Fortran installation is likely to use three or four main commands which activate appropriate batch files; one to set the correct system environment, one to compile a Fortran source file, another to link the object file to the library routines, and yet another to quit the system and reset the system environment to its former settings.

10

Do consult your computer department for the precise form of these commands as they will most certainly be different from those given above. The principle, however, is the same.

——————————————— **Problem 1.1** ———————————————

Write a program, using the READ statement, which assigns three numbers to the variables Days, Hours and Minutes and then calculates and prints the total number of minutes involved. Compile and execute the program.

Exercises

1. Write the following numbers as Fortran real constants.

   256   −43,000 10^{12} $−10^{-16}$ 0.000000492

2. The following are unacceptable integer constants. Why?

   −234.   23,400   .1E−12   −.2E10   2.379427

3. The following are unacceptable real constants. Why?

   −10,000   1E−55   2.379−E12   −.22E5.1   9870

4. The following are unacceptable names of integer variables. why?

   JOBLESS   ABACUS   5MARKS   *JARS   K34.5

5. The following are unacceptable names for real variables. why?

   ALPHABET   8BOX   NUMBER   FORM-6   A+B

6. The following assignment statements contain at least one error. Identify them.

   ALPHA = 5.X+BETA
   SQUARE = 1.55/−2.44*G**2
   VALUE-3.96 = X**1.6
   3.14 = PI
   DENOMINATOR = X**N/M
   X = (A+6)**2
   −ZETA = A+B
   NUMBER = K**X
   ROW = 16.5K+1
   COLUMN = 2*−X+1

7. Write a program, using the READ statement, which can convert degrees Fahrenheit (F) to degrees Celsius (C). Use the relationship

   Degrees Celsius = (Degrees Fahrenheit − 32) * 5/9

2. PRIORITIES & OUTPUT CONTROL

Priority in arithmetic operations

The calculations in the AVERAGE program of the previous chapter are performed in the second and third executable statements. Combining them into one statement, we could write

$$X = (A + B + C)/3.0 \qquad (\textbf{Not } X = A + B + C/3.0)$$

It is important that the numerator of this expression is in brackets. If it were not, Fortran would evaluate first C/3.0 and then add to it A + B, which would give the wrong result. This is due to an in-built system of priorities, shown below.

───────── **Arithmetic Operators and their Priority** ─────────

Fortran symbol	Example	Priority	Function
( )	(A + B)/X	1	Parenthesized operation
**	A**N	2	Raise A to the Nth power
*	A*X	3	Multiplication
/	A/X	3	Division
+	A + X	4	Addition
−	A − X	4	Subtraction

On evaluating expressions, Fortran performs arithmetical operations in the order of priority indicated in the table. Expressions in parentheses are evaluated first. Nested groups in parentheses are evaluated beginning with the innermost grouping and working outwards.

Fortran cannot accept two consecutive operators. For example, A*-B is illegal. It must be written as A*(-B). Through the use of parentheses, the order of priority of execution, and therefore the final value of an expression, can be changed. If a line has an expression which contains several operators of equal priority, Fortran will evaluate it from left to right.

Let us examine how a complicated expression such as

    Y =(A+B*X)**2/C-D*X**3

is evaluated. We assume that the values of A, B, C, D and X are known. First the parenthesized portion of the expression will be evaluated. Within these parentheses the multiplication has a higher priority and therefore it will be evaluated first. Then, A will be added to it, resulting in a numerical value to which we will assign the letter Z. Now the expression is reduced to the following:

    Y=Z**2/C-D*X**3

The above has two exponential expressions, the leftmost of which is evaluated first. Writing Z1 for the result of Z**2 and X1 for the result of X**3, the expression is now reduced to

    Y=Z1/C-D*X1

Again, since division and multiplication have the same priority, the leftmost expression is evaluated first. Finally, the result of the multiplication is taken away from the result of the division and assigned to Y. All this procedure is, of course, carried out automatically by Fortran, but if you intend to use complicated mathematical expressions you must be familiar with it.

The assignment statement
Note that what appears as an equation above is, in fact, an assignment statement and not an algebraic identity. As long as the values of variables on the right of an equals sign are known, the calculated result will be assigned to the variable on the left of the equals sign. As an example, consider the following short program.

14

```
       1        2        3
1234567890123456789012345678901   ---  column position
C EXAMPLE OF ACCUMULATION
      K=0
      K=K+1
      PRINT *, K
      STOP
      END
```

The second executable statement would be meaningless had it
been an algebraic expression. In computing terms the statement
states 'take the present value in K, add one to it and store the result
in K'. When this statement is executed, the value of K (set in the
previous statement) is zero and adding one to it results in a new
value of K equal to one.

───────────────── **Problem 2.1** ─────────────────

In each of the following expressions, the variables used have the
following values:

Variable	A	B	C	D	E	F	G
Value	5.0	3.0	8.0	4.0	7.0	2.0	6.0

Use paper and pencil and a calculator to work out the correct
answer to the expressions given below. To arrive at the final answer, calculate all intermediate steps in the order dictated by the
priority procedure.

```
X1=A*B**E+F
X2=A*B**(E+F)
X3=A*B/C*D
X4=A*B/(C*D)
X5=A+B*G+C*G**2+D*G**3
X6=(A+B)*G+C*G**2+D*G**3
X7=(A**F+(B-1.0/C)**F)**0.5
X8=(A**F+B-1.0/C**F)**0.5
X9=A/B**2-C*D/((E+F)+G**3)
```

Declared integer or real variable types

We saw in the previous chapter that variables whose first letter begins with I, J, K, L, M or N (remember the word INteger) are implied integer while those beginning with any other letter are implied to be real. This initial first letter convention can be over-written with the use of declaration statements.

To declare variables to be of integer type, use the INTEGER statement which consists of the word INTEGER followed by the variable names separated by commas. Similarly, to declare variables to be of real type, use the REAL statement. Such type declaration statements must appear before any executable statements. The following example will help to clarify the use of declaration statements.

```
         1         2         3         4         5
12345678901234567890123456789012345678901234567890
C CALCULATE PERCENT
      REAL NUMBER
      PRINT *, 'ENTER A NUMBER'
      READ *, NUMBER
      PRINT *, 'ENTER %'
      READ *, RATE
      VALUE=NUMBER*RATE/100.0
      PRINT *, RATE, ' % OF ', NUMBER, ' = ', VALUE
      STOP
      END
```

Note the first statement after the comment line is the declaration statement 'REAL NUMBER' which causes the stated variable to be treated as a real variable throughout the program, even though it starts with the letter N. The statement must appear prior to any other executable statements, such as PRINT, READ or indeed any assignment statement.

On executing the program, Fortran writes

```
ENTER A NUMBER
415
ENTER %
15

        15.000000 % OF      415.000000 =      62.250000

Stop - Program terminated.
```

16

Note that by including in the program strategically placed PRINT statements we make the interaction between computer and user more friendly. The user is prompted for input and the result of the calculation is printed out with an intelligible message.

Enter this program in your computer and execute it. Notice for yourself how the output appears on the screen. In your case, the spacing might differ from the above if you are using a different Fortran compiler. Remember that when using the free format PRINT statement the output can differ from compiler to compiler, as it is dependent on the original design criteria which were under the sole discretion of the person who wrote the compiler in the first place.

Formatted output

The limitations encountered when using a free format PRINT statement can be overcome with the incorporation of the FORMAT statement within the PRINT statement. This gives us full control on the layout of the output, as well as the form in which the numbers printed out will appear. To illustrate the mechanism, the PERCENT program is reproduced below, but with the incorporation of the FORMAT statement in the last PRINT statement.

```
          1         2         3         4         5
 123456789012345678901234567890123456789012345678901234567890
 C CALCULATE PERCENT
       REAL NUMBER
       PRINT *, 'ENTER A NUMBER'
       READ *, NUMBER
       PRINT *, 'ENTER %'
       READ *, RATE
       VALUE=NUMBER*RATE/100.0
       PRINT 10, RATE, NUMBER, VALUE
    10 FORMAT (1X, F5.2,' % OF ',F6.2,' = ',F5.2)
       STOP
       END
```

Note that the PRINT statement now has a number in place of the asterisk of the previous version of the program. It specifies the label of FORMAT statement under which the three variables RATE, NUMBER and VALUE are to be printed. The FORMAT statement is preceded with a label number which corresponds to that given within the PRINT statement, and is followed by a parenthesized list of items separated by commas.

The first item in the format list is the specification 1X. It is a control code which we can send to the printer to control horizontal spacing and we will use it from now on as the first format specification with every FORMAT statement. The precise effect it has on the output will be discussed later when we examine in some detail horizontal and vertical spacing control codes.

The next item in the list is the format specification F5.2 which means 'print the corresponding variable in the PRINT list in a floating point specification, in a field of 6 characters with 2 digits after the decimal point'. There are three such format specifications within the FORMAT statement, each corresponding to the variable appearing within the PRINT statement. Thus, the contents of variable RATE are printed in F5.2 format, that of NUMBER in F6.2 and that of VALUE in F5.2. There is a one-to-one correspondence between the variables appearing in the PRINT statement and the format specification appearing in the FORMAT statement. In between the format specifications we can print other explanatory information, provided it is within apostrophes and separated from other items in the list by comas.

Modify the PERCENT program in your computer to incorporate the formatted PRINT statement. On execution you should get the following output

```
ENTER A NUMBER
415
ENTER %
15
15.00 % OF 415.00 = 62.25

Stop - Program terminated
```

which provides a much tidier output than that of the previously free formatted printout. Note that if we chose a very large number as the first input, it will not fit within the field width chosen in the last PRINT statement. In that case, the computer prints a row of asterisks to indicate that the number is too large to be printed out in the given field.

Numeric format specifications

The three most commonly used numeric format specifications are:

Iw	or	nIw	for Integer numbers
Fw.d	or	nFw.d	for Floating point numbers
Ew.d	or	nEw.d	for Exponential numbers

where

w   is a positive integer giving the number of characters in the external representation. It should be large enough to include sign, digits, decimal point and a four-character exponent multiplier,

d   is a positive integer giving the number of digits in the fractional part, and

n   is the number of times the field is repeated

In all cases, the number is considered to be right justified within the field specified. Character positions to the left of the number are filled with blanks. Thus, an output using the w specifications can be used to provide appropriate spacing between successive numbers in the same output line.

The following example will serve to illustrate the above format specifications.

```
          1         2         3         4         5
 12345678901234567890123456789012345678901234567890
 C THREE OUTPUT SPECIFICATIONS
        REAL NUMBER
        INTEGER TRUNC
        PRINT *, 'ENTER A NUMBER'
        READ *, NUMBER
        TRUNC=NUMBER
 C VARIABLE TRUNC HOLDS THE TRUNCATED VALUE OF NUMBER
        PRINT 10
   10   FORMAT (1X,
      & 'THREE KINDS OF FORMATTED REPRESENTATION')
        PRINT 20
   20   FORMAT (1X,
      & 'TRUNCATED     FLOATING POINT     EXPONENTIAL')
        PRINT 30, TRUNC, NUMBER, NUMBER
   30   FORMAT (1X, I9, F19.3, E16.6)
        STOP
        END
```

Enter the program in your computer using the source filename THREEFORM.FOR and compile it. On execution, the following output should appear under the appropriate column position.

```
          1         2         3         4         5
12345678901234567890123456789012345678901234567890
ENTER A NUMBER
256.512
THREE KINDS OF FORMATTED REPRESENTATION
TRUNCATED      FLOATING POINT      EXPONENTIAL
      256             256.512      .256512E+03
```

Note that the column ruler is not part of the program. It has been included here to make it easier for you.

In the program, the entered numeric value of 256.512 is associated with the variable NUMBER. As this variable name starts with the letter N (which normally signifies an integer), we declared it a real variable with the REAL statement because we need to be able to enter decimal numbers. Further, in the assignment statement following the READ, the value of variable NUMBER is assigned to variable TRUNC (short for 'truncated'). Again, as the first letter of TRUNC starts with T (which normally signifies a real variable), and here we want it to hold the truncated part of the number, we declare TRUNC an integer with the INTEGER statement.

The next two PRINT statements, which are associated with FORMATs 10 and 20, provide headings for the output. Note the line continuation symbol '&' on the 6th column of the line following each of these FORMAT statements. It allows the line with the '&' symbol to be treated by the compiler as part of the previous line. Any character in the 6th column will have the same effect. We chose the '&' symbol as it cannot be confused with arithmetic operators or any other characters normally found in Fortran statements.

The final PRINT statement causes the value of TRUNC (an integer variable) to be printed in integer representation (I9 in FORMAT 30), and the value of the repeated variable NUMBER to be printed in two different forms; first in floating point representation (F19.3 in the FORMAT), and second in exponential representation (E16.6). Note that the field widths (9 for I, 19 for F and 16 for E) are contiguous and were chosen here so that the printed values appear right justified under the last letter of their respective heading.

20

───────────────── **Problem 2.2** ─────────────────

Write a program to read in a positive floating point number into a variable called VALUE, place the integral part of it into variable INTEG, and the fractional part of it into variable FRACT. Print out the original number, and the integral and fractional parts of it under appropriate headings.

───

The solution of the above problem could easily be based on the program THREEFORM. Try it.

Output spacing controls

Horizontal spacing:

Horizontal spacing of printed output can be achieved with the use of the X-FORMAT. We have already used the 1X specification as the first item in a FORMAT list without explaining the precise effect it had. This will be put right shortly when we discuss vertical spacing.

The general form of the X-FORMAT is as follows:

    nX

where n is the number of characters to be skipped.

As an example, we could re-write the FORMAT statements 20 and 30 of the THREEFORM program as follows:

```
20   FORMAT (1X, 'TRUNCATED', 5X, 'FLOATING POINT',
     & 5X, 'EXPONENTIAL')

30   FORMAT (1X, I9, 9X, F10.3, E16.6)
```

The X-FORMAT specification in Fortran, is similar to the SPC() statement in BASIC. It allows the insertion of spaces between output lists. It can immediately be seen that it is easier to use this specification rather than attempt to appropriately space out words within a single pair of apostrophes, or try to work out the field width of numeric specifications so that output can be printed on an exact position.

Re-compiling the THREEFORM program with the above changes and executing it, will give the same output as before.

Vertical spacing:
Control codes can be sent to the printer to control line spacing. For example, if we include as the first item in a FORMAT list a single space enclosed in apostrophes (' '), it forces the printing of what follows in single spacing. In fact, the printer is expecting to receive such a code from each FORMAT statement for each printed line, and if it does not, it simply takes the first blank character preceding a number or caption for its own use. As this destroys tabulation, we supplied the printer with a throw away character, a space, using the 1X specification.

There are other control codes which add to the flexibility in designing the way output can be presented to the user. The full range together with their meaning is shown below.

Control code	Meaning
Blank	Single space before printing
0 (zero)	Double space before printing
1	Skip to top of next page
+	Suppress spacing — overprint

Another way of obtaining vertical spacing control is through the use of slashes in a FORMAT statement. If N consecutive slashes are placed at the beginning or end of a FORMAT statement, N blank lines are written either before or after the described item, whichever the case might be. If consecutive slashes are used anywhere else in the FORMAT statement, the number of blank lines inserted is N-1.

The following example will help to illustrate the above point.

```
          1         2         3         4         5
12345678901234567890123456789012345678901234567890
C PROGRAM TO ILLUSTRATE SPACING CONTROLS
      A=1.0
      B=2.0
      C=3.0
      D=4.0
      PRINT 10
10    FORMAT (1X, 'FIRST RECORD')
      PRINT 20, A, B, C, D
20    FORMAT (1X,//F10.1,F10.1//,F10.1,F10.1//)
      PRINT 30
30    FORMAT (1X, 'LAST RECORD')
      STOP
      END
```

On execution, the following output will be displayed.

```
         1         2         3         4         5
12345678901234567890123456789012345678901234567890
FIRST RECORD


     1.0       2.0

     3.0       4.0


   LAST RECORD
```

Note that there are two blank lines between the caption FIRST
RECORD and the first row of numbers, one blank line between the
two rows of numbers, and two blank lines between the second
row of numbers and the caption LAST RECORD. Also note that
the two rows of numbers are shifted to the left by one character.
This is because the format specification 1X in FORMAT 20 has no
effect on the actual numeric lines. It is lost with the printing of the
first blank line. The FORMAT should have been written instead as

```
20   FORMAT (//1X,F10.1,F10.1//,1X,F10.1,F10.1//)
```

so that it precedes the non-blank lines.

Repetition of format codes
As written in the above example, FORMAT 20 has an obvious
repetition. We used two pairs of F10.1 specifications to print out
the four variables A, B, C and D. One way of shortening the statement would be to write it as follows:

```
20   FORMAT (//1X,2F10.1//,1X,2F10.1//)
```

The 'repeated' specification (2F10.1) causes print of each pair of
numbers for each row. It means 'two floating point numbers, each
in a field of 10 characters with one digit after the decimal point',
which is correct as it preserves the one-to-one correspondence
between variables and their respective format specification.

Indeed, we could go one step further and eliminate another repetition by writing

23

```
20    FORMAT (2(//1X,2F10.1)//)
```

which allows the inner bracket specification (//2F10.1) to be repeated twice.

Be careful when writing format specifications in such a compact way. If the total number of variables in the PRINT list exceeds the numeric format specifications supplied, then the FORMAT will be repeated which will automatically provide unwanted vertical spacing of the output. For example, had we written

```
20    FORMAT (2(//1X,F10.1)//)
```

we would have got the following output:

```
         1         2         3         4         5
12345678901234567890123456789012345678901234567890
FIRST RECORD



      1.0


      2.0



      3.0


      4.0


 LAST RECORD
```

Note that there are two blank lines between FIRST RECORD and the value of A (as before), but the value of B is printed by repeating the specification of the inner bracket of the FORMAT statement due to the repetition counter 2 which appears infront of the bracket. This has the effect of executing (//F10.1) again, which results in one blank line between the value of variable A and that of B. After printing the value of B, the final two slash codes of the format are executed, giving two blank lines. On attempting, however, to print the value of C and finding that there are no more numeric specifications left in FORMAT 20, the whole format statement is repeated. This starts with the printing of two additional blank lines before printing the value of C, and so on. The result will not be what you had intended.

24

───────────────── **Problem 2.3** ─────────────────

Write a program to calculate the cost of electricity at 5.5 pence per unit between quarterly meter readings LOWVAL and HIVAL which represent the 'low meter reading value' and the 'high meter reading value'. The flat quarterly charge, irrespective of units used, is 8.85.

Use the READ statement to assign values to LOWVAL, HIVAL, and the assignment statement to assign values to UCOST and FRATE, representing 'unit cost' and 'flat rate'.

───

The formatted WRITE statement
Formats can be specified within a WRITE statement in the same way as we have used them with the PRINT statement.

Where the PRINT statement in a program section could be written as

```
        PRINT 20, A,B,C
    20  FORMAT (3F10.3)
```

the equivalent WRITE statement would take the form

```
        WRITE (6,20) A,B,C
    20  FORMAT (3F10.3)
```

The second number within the parentheses of the WRITE statement refers to the FORMAT label which, as before, describes how data are to be presented, while the first number refers to the unit on which data is to appear. Note the comma separating the two numbers within the parentheses, and the omission of a comma between the closing parenthesis and the first variable in the list.

25

Exercises

1. The values of six variables are to be printed on one line. Variables A and B are to be in 12 printing positions each with two digits after the decimal point, variables K and L are to be in 10 printing positions each, and variables X and Y are to be in 16 printing positions each with exponents and six digits after the decimal point. Write appropriate statements to achieve the layout of this print.

2. Modify the AVERAGE program (see Chapter 1), which uses the READ statement to enter three numbers in variables A, B and C and calculates their average value, by incorporating the X-FORMAT specification so that the output appears in tabular form, under the appropriate headings as shown below.

   VALUES: A   B   C   AVERAGE

3. Modify the program of Problem 1.1, by using appropriate FORMAT spacing controls so that the output appears in tabular form, under appropriate headings as shown below.

   DAYS   HOURS   MINUTES   TOTAL_MINUTES

4. Modify the program of Problem 2.2, by using the slash control for formatting output spacing so as to allow two blank lines to be printed between the end of data entry and the caption describing the numeric values printed under it.

5. Write a program to read a number and then calculate and print under suitable headings, the original number and the discounted values at 12.5%, 15% and 17.5% of the original value.

6. Write a program which calculates the area of a circle, the surface area of a sphere and the volume of a sphere, given the radius R.

   The output should appear on one line under appropriate captions.

26

3. CONTROL OF PROGRAM FLOW

The DO loop

The DO and CONTINUE statements are used to mark the beginning and ending points of program loops. Any statements between the DO and its correspondingly labelled CONTINUE statement will be executed repeatedly according to the conditions supplied by the 'control variable' within the DO statement. To illustrate the point, a simple example is given below.

```
          1         2         3         4         5
123456789012345678901234567890123456789012345678901234567890
C EXAMPLE USING THE DO LOOP
       DO 100 K=1,5,1
          PRINT *, K
  100  CONTINUE
       STOP
       END
```

In the DO statement, the control variable K is assigned the value 1 which is increased repeatedly by the last number in the statement until it reaches 5 (the middle of the three numbers following the control varable K). It thus has the values 1, 2, 3, 4 and 5. Since it cannot have these values simultaneously, a loop is formed beginning with the DO statement and ending with an appropriately labelled CONTINUE. The label of the CONTINUE (100 in this case), also appears within the DO statement (DO 100). The statements within the loop are re-executed five times, each time with a new value for K.

The CONTINUE statement does nothing; it merely acts as the end of the loop, which in fact does not have to be a CONTINUE statement. The end of a DO loop could be a PRINT or a READ statement, appropriately labelled. However, for the sake of simplicity we will use CONTINUE for a while. The statements enclosed within the DO loop are executed until such time as the value of the control variable K exceeds its final assigned value of 5. When this happens, program control passes to whatever statement follows the CONTINUE statement (in this case STOP).

The control variable within a DO loop can be assigned integer, real or double precision values, provided the control variable name has been declared appropriately.

The 'first', 'last' and 'step increment' values of the control variable could be assigned via variable names, as follows:

```
DO 100 K=FIRST,LAST,STEP
```

provided all four variables are of the same numeric type, for example, all integer or all real.

The following program makes use of the DO loop as well as an accumulator to find the sum of a list of numbers.

```
          1         2         3         4         5
12345678901234567890123456789012345678901234567890
C SUM OF N NUMBERS USING A DO LOOP
      PRINT *, 'ENTER NUMBER OF VALUES TO BE SUMMED'
      READ *, N
      SUM=0
      DO 100 K=1,N,1
        PRINT *, 'ENTER VALUE NO.',K
        READ *, VALUE
        SUM=SUM+VALUE
  100   CONTINUE
      PRINT *, 'SUM OF ',N, 'NUMBERS = ',SUM
      STOP
      END
```

On executing this program, N is assigned the value 5, by the READ statement, which is the total number of entries requiring summation. The accumulator SUM is then zeroed, and a DO loop is set up between the DO statement and the CONTINUE statement labelled as 100. Note that we have indented the statements in between the DO and CONTINUE to make reading of the program easier.

Within the loop, each number is read into VALUE and accumulated into SUM. Once the loop is completed, SUM holds the sum of all the numbers. On execution of the last PRINT statement, Fortran will write

```
SUM OF 5 NUMBERS = 104.3
```

provided you supplied the program with the following five numbers: 20.5, 21.3, 20.8, 20.6, 21.1.

The DO loop step modifier

In the last example, the step modifier was equal to + 1. When this is the case, the step modifier can be omitted and the DO loop can be written as

```
DO 100 K=1,N
```

in which case it is assumed that the step increment is equal to + 1. If the desired step value, which can be anything, is not equal to + 1, the step modifier must be included. For example

```
          1         2         3         4         5
12345678901234567890123456789012345678901234567890
C CONVERT INCHES TO CENTIMETRES
      REAL INCHES
      PRINT *, 'INCHES    ', '    CENTIMETRES'
      DO 100 INCHES=5,20,5
        CENTIM=2.54*INCHES
        PRINT *, INCHES, CENTIM
100   CONTINUE
      STOP
      END
```

will convert 5, 10, 15 and 20 inches into centimetres. The output should be (with a few more zeros) as follows:

INCHES	CENTIMETRES
5.00	12.70
10.00	25.40
15.00	38.10
20.00	50.80

A negative step modifier is legal in Fortran 77. For example

```
      DO 10 J=5,1,-1
      PRINT *, J
10    CONTINUE
      STOP
      END
```

will print the values 5, 4, 3, 2 and 1.

For positive step values, the loop is executed so long as the control variable is less than or equal to its final value. For negative step values the loop continues as long as the control variable is greater than or equal to its final value.

Nested DO loops

DO-CONTINUE statements can be nested to allow the programming of loops within loops as shown in the example below.

```
             1         2         3         4         5
    1234567890123456789012345678901234567890123456789 0
    C NESTED DO LOOPS
          DO 10 K=1,2
            PRINT 100, K
    100     FORMAT (1X, 'OUTER LOOP WITH K =',I2)
            DO 20 L=1,3
              PRINT 200, L
    200       FORMAT (11X, 'INNER LOOP WITH L =',I2)
    20      CONTINUE
    10    CONTINUE
          STOP
          END
```

On executing this program, two loops are set up as follows:

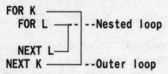

The outer loop is initialized with K = 1 and immediately the inner nested loop is executed 3 times. Then the control variable K is incremented by 1, so that now K = 2 and the nested loop is executed another 3 times. The output of this program is as follows:

```
OUTER LOOP WITH K = 1
            INNER LOOP WITH L = 1
            INNER LOOP WITH L = 2
            INNER LOOP WITH L = 3

OUTER LOOP WITH K = 2
            INNER LOOP WITH L = 1
            INNER LOOP WITH L = 2
            INNER LOOP WITH L = 3
```

Additional levels of nesting are possible. However, deep nesting is costly in terms of memory space. Fig. 3.1 shows some loop configurations, the first five of which are examples of allowable loops, while the sixth is not. Lines joining DO-CONTINUE statements must not cross.

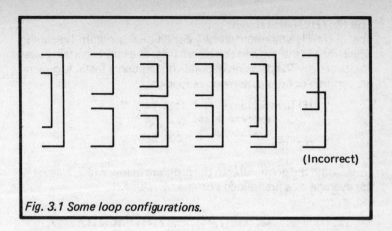

(Incorrect)

Fig. 3.1 Some loop configurations.

WARNING

No statement within the DO loop must be allowed to change the parameters of the loop. Those of you who are familiar with BASIC might be tempted to terminate a DO loop by changing the final value of the control variable from within the loop itself. Do *not* do this as Fortran does not work this way. It simply notes the parameters of the DO loop the first time round and ignores any subsequent attempts to change them. For this very reason, any attempt to bypass the DO statement will result in failure.

——————————— **Problem 3.1** ———————————

Compound interest can be calculated using the formula

$$A = P * (1 + R/100)^n$$

where P is the original money lent, A is what it amounts to in n years at R per cent per annum interest.

Write a program to calculate the amount of money owed after n years, where n changes from 1 to 15 in yearly increments, if the money lent originally is £5,000 and the interest rate remains constant throughout this period at 11.5%. Use the FORMAT statement to restrict calculated values to two decimal places and tabulate the results.

The IF..THEN statement

The IF..THEN statement allows conditional program branching which means that we can decide whether to execute certain statements or not. The decision depends on relational tests. In general we can think of the statement as follows:

```
IF ({ relational test is true} ) THEN
   {   execute these   }
   {     statements     }
END IF
```

To illustrate the point, refer to the program below which calcuates the average of a predefined number of values.

```
            1         2         3         4         5
   12345678901234567890123456789012345678901234567890
C AVERAGE OF N NUMBERS
      PRINT *, 'ENTER NUMBER OF VALUES TO BE AVERAGED'
      READ *, N
      IF (N .GT. 0) THEN
         SUM=0
         TOTAL=N
         DO 100 K=1,N
            PRINT *, 'ENTER VALUE NO.',K
            READ *, VALUE
            SUM=SUM+VALUE
  100    CONTINUE
         AVER=SUM/TOTAL
         PRINT *, 'AVERAGE OF ',N, ' NUMBERS = ',AVER
      END IF
      STOP
      END
```

When Fortran encounters this IF statement, it compares the value of the variable N with the constant appearing after the relational operator (in this case the .GT. which stands for 'greater than' - more about this later). If the test condition is met, the trailer of the IF statement is executed (in this case all the statements between the IF and END IF statements. If, however, the test condition is not met, the statement following the END IF statement is executed (in this case STOP). The IF statement here acts as a guard against an attempt to enter a zero for N which would result in a zero being divided by zero when working out the average.

Relational operators within IF statements
The table below shows all the relational operators allowed within an IF statement.

──────────── **Table of Relational Operators** ────────────

Fortran symbol	Example	Meaning
.EQ.	A .EQ. B	A equal to B
.LT.	A .LT. B	A less than B
.LE.	A .LE. B	A less than or equal to B
.GT.	A .GT. B	A greater than B
.GE.	A .GE. B	A greater than or equal to B
.NE.	A .NE. B	A not equal to B

The dots on either side of the letters making up the relational operators are part of the definition of these operators and must be included.

The power of the IF statement is increased considerably by the combination of several relational expressions with the logical operators

.AND.   .OR.   .NOT.

We can write the statement

        IF (X .GT. 3.0 .AND. M .EQ. 5) THEN

which states that only if both combinations are met will the trailer of the IF statement be executed. Note that all logical testing is within brackets and that real variables are compared with real numbers, while integer variables are compared with integer numbers.

Another example is:

```
IF (X .GT. 3.0 .OR. M .EQ. 5) THEN
```

which states that when either is true, then the trailer of the IF
statement will be executed. Finally, the statement

```
IF (.NOT. (X .LT. 12.0)) THEN
```

has the same effect as

```
IF (X .GE. 12.0) THEN
```

The IF...THEN...ELSE statement

In many cases we have to perform an IF statement twice over to
detect which of two similar conditions is true. This is illustrated
below.

```
          1         2         3         4         5
1234567890123456789012345678901234567890123456789
C THE TWO IF STATEMENTS
      PRINT *, 'ENTER A NUMBER WITHIN 1 TO 99'
      READ *, N
      IF (N .LT. 10) THEN
         PRINT *, 'ONE DIGIT NUMBER'
      END IF
      IF (N .GT. 9) THEN
         PRINT *, 'TWO DIGIT NUMBER'
      END IF
      STOP
      END
```

A more advanced version of the IF statement allows both actions
to be inserted in its trailer. An example of this is incorporated in the
modified program below.

```
          1         2         3         4         5
1234567890123456789012345678901234567890123456789
C USE OF THE IF..THEN..ELSE STATEMENTS
      PRINT *, 'ENTER A NUMBER WITHIN 1 TO 99'
      READ *, N
      IF (N .LT. 10) THEN
         PRINT *, 'ONE DIGIT NUMBER'
      ELSE
         PRINT *, 'TWO DIGIT NUMBER'
      END IF
      STOP
      END
```

34

Execute the THEN ELSE program and supply numbers between 1 and 99. Obviously, if you type in numbers greater than 99 the program will not function correctly in its present form. But assuming that you have obeyed the message and typed 50 the second PRINT statement in the trailer of the IF statement (after the ELSE) will be executed. If the number entered was less than 10, the first PRINT statement after THEN would be executed.

The GOTO statement

The GOTO statement provides unconditional program branching; it causes an immediate jump to an indicated statement label. Program execution continues sequentially again, beginning with the line just reached. To illustrate this statement we re-write the THEN ELSE program below.

```
          1         2         3         4         5
123456789012345678901234567890123456789012345678901234567890
C USE OF THE GOTO STATEMENT
   10    PRINT *, 'ENTER A NUMBER WITHIN 1 TO 99'
         READ *, N
         IF (N .GE. 1 .AND. N .LE. 99) THEN
           IF (N .LT. 10) THEN
             PRINT *, 'ONE DIGIT NUMBER'
           ELSE
             PRINT *, 'TWO DIGIT NUMBER'
           END IF
           GOTO 10
         END IF
         STOP
         END
```

In the above program the GOTO statement sends program execution back to label 10 which allows us to go through the program as many times as we like. However, we must also provide a mechanism for stopping the program which, in this case, is achieved with the addition of the first IF statement. This tests to see if the number entered is within the allowable range; if it is, the inner statements are executed, otherwise program execution stops. Thus, to stop this program type 0 (zero) in response to the caption

`'ENTER A NUMBER WITHIN 1 TO 99'.`

Fortran 77 does not provide loop statements similar to the REPEAT-UNTIL or the WHILE-ENDWHILE variety. However, the intelligent use of the GOTO statement can simulate these quite adequately. In the above program, we have actually simulated the WHILE-ENDWHILE loop.

35

Simple data sorting

The program below allows us to enter two numbers, tests to find out which is the larger of the two and prints them in descending order.

```
        1         2         3         4         5
12345678901234567890123456789012345678901234567890
C TWO NUMBER SORT
10    PRINT *, 'ENTER TWO NUMBERS'
      READ *, A, B
      IF (A .GE. 0.0) THEN
        IF (A .GE. B) THEN
          PRINT *, A, B
        ELSE
          PRINT *, B, A
        END IF
        GOTO 10
      END IF
      STOP
      END
```

The program can be stopped by entering a negative value for A. Otherwise, A is compared with B and the appropriate PRINT statement in the trailer of the IF statement is executed.

The sorting problem becomes more complicated, however, if instead of two numbers we introduce a third one. For two number sorting we had two possible PRINT statements (the number of possible permutations being $1*2=2$). For three number sorting however, the total number of PRINT statements becomes six (the total possible permutations being equal to $1*2*3=6$). The combinations are (A,B,C), (A,C,B); (C,A,B), (C,B,A), (B,C,A) and (B,A,C).

A slight variation of the IF statement reduces the total number of statements required to solve this problem. We can, for example, ask whether A is greater than B and B greater than C in one statement, thus combining two statements into one. This form of IF statement is:

```
IF (A .GT. B .AND. B .GT. C) THEN
  PRINT *, A, B, C
END IF
```

The trailer of this IF statement will only be executed if, and only if, both A is greater than B and also B is greater than C.

36

Returning to the problem of sorting three numbers, if we were to pursue the suggested method, we would require five IF statements to PRINT six combinations of A,B,C. The logic suggested in dealing with the problem would result in a very inefficient program.

Here is a way in which, with only three IF statements and one PRINT statement, the same solution to the three-number sorting problem can be achieved. It uses a different logic and it is explained here with the help of three imaginary playing cards (see Fig. 3.2). Assume that you are holding these cards in your hand and you wish to arrange them in descending order. Look at the front two (Fig. 3.2a) and arrange them so that the highest value appears in front. Now look at the back two (Fig. 3.2b) and arrange them so that the highest of these two is now in front. Obviously, if the highest card had been at the back, in the first instance, it would by now have moved to the middle position (as shown in Fig. 3.2c), so a repeat of the whole procedure is necessary to ensure that the highest card is at the front (Fig. 3.2d).

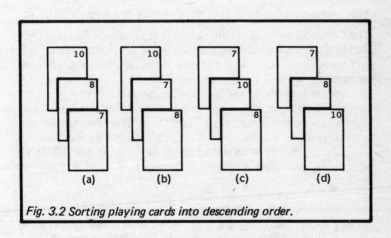

Fig. 3.2 Sorting playing cards into descending order.

The program below achieves this.

```
          1         2         3         4         5
 12345678901234567890123456789012345678901234567890
 C THREE NUMBER SORT
       PRINT *, 'ENTER THREE NUMBERS'
       READ *, A, B, C
   10  IF (A .LT. B .OR. B .LT. C) THEN
          IF (A .LT. B) THEN
            TEMP=A
            A=B
            B=TEMP
          END IF
          IF (B .LT. C) THEN
            TEMP=B
            B=C
            C=TEMP
          END IF
          GOTO 10
       END IF
       PRINT *, A, B, C
       STOP
       END
```

Type this program into the computer under the name NRSORT.

The following actions are indicated: If the value in A is less than
that in B, exchange them so that the value of A is now stored in B
and the value of B is now stored in A. Note, however, that were we
to put the value of B into A, we should lose the number stored in A
(by overwriting). We therefore transfer the contents of A to a temporary (TEMP) variable, then transfer the contents of B to A and
finally transfer the contents of TEMP to B. The second rotation,
necessary when B is less than C, is achieved in a similar manner.
The whole process is repeated (with the help of the GOTO 10
statement), until both A is greater or equal to B and B is greater or
equal to C.

———————————————— Problem 3.2 ————————————————
Modify the NRSORT program so that it loops in such a way as to
allow repeated execution of the code for different sets of input
numbers. Also provide a method of stopping execution.

The LOGICAL statement

The declaration statement

```
LOGICAL FLAG
```

will cause the variable FLAG to be declared as a logical variable. A logical variable does not obey the initial letter naming convention.

A logical variable can hold one or other of two values represented by the logical constants .TRUE. and .FALSE. which may be assigned in a logical assignment statement such as

```
FLAG=.TRUE.
```

or

```
FLAG=.FALSE.
```

A logical expression may be a relational expression such as

```
SWITCH=A .GE. 20.0
```

In this case SWITCH is set to .TRUE. or .FALSE. depending on the truth value of the relationship on the right. Thus, logical variables enable the recording of a certain condition and its subsequent test. Having given SWITCH a value, the logical IF statement can be used as follows:

```
IF (SWITCH) THEN
   ---
   ---
   ---
END IF
```

In a relational expression (such as that for SWITCH above) we can not only use relational operators such as .GE., but also combine them with the logical operators .AND., .OR. and .NOT., the latter reversing the truth value of the expression it operates on. For example, the statement

```
SWITCH=A .GT. B .AND. .NOT. FLAG
```

will cause SWITCH to take the value .TRUE. only when A is greater than B and FLAG is .FALSE., if FLAG had been defined as .TRUE. in a previous logical statement.

The computed GOTO statement

This is a statement which allows program execution to be diverted to one of several lines. It should only be used when a program is distinctly divided to separate sections. The statement is written as follows:

```
GOTO (100,200,300), INDEX
```

where INDEX is an unsigned integer variable. If the value of INDEX at the time of execution is 1, it branches to the statement with the first label within the GOTO argument list (in this case 100); when INDEX is equal to 2, it branches to the second (in this case label 200), and so on. If INDEX has a value less than 1 or greater than the total number of label numbers in the trailer of the statement, Fortran passess program control to the next statement following the computed GOTO statement.

As an example, consider the program below which can find either the square root, the square or the cube of any number.

```
          1         2         3         4         5
12345678901234567890123456789012345678901234567890
C  USE OF COMPUTED GOTO STATEMENT
        PRINT *, 'NUMBER PLEASE'
        READ *, VALUE
        PRINT *, 'SQUAREROOT/SQUARE/CUBE/END (1/2/3/4)'
        READ *, K
        GOTO (50,100,150,10),K
   10   STOP
   50   SQROOT=VALUE**0.5
        PRINT *,'THE SQUARE ROOT OF ',VALUE,' = ',SQROOT
        STOP
  100   SQUARE=VALUE**2
        PRINT *,'THE SQUARE OF ',VALUE,' = ',SQUARE
        STOP
  150   CUBE=VALUE**3
        PRINT *,'THE CUBE OF ',VALUE,' = ',CUBE
        STOP
        END
```

To stop this program type 4 in response to the prompt from the second PRINT statement.

Write a program that can carry out any of the following conversions:

(a) gallons into litres   (1 gallon = 4.54609 litres)
(b) feet into metres   (1 foot = 0.3048 metres)
(c) pounds into kilograms   (1 pound = 0.453592 kilogram)

Use assignment statements to enter the conversion constants into the computer, and the READ statement for entering the number to be converted and the type of conversion required.

Exercises

1. Write a program using the DO loop to calculate the squares and cubes of numbers from 1 to 10 inclusive. The results should appear in tabular form under appropriate headings.

2. Modify the compound interest program (see Problem 3.1) so that the annual interest rate is increased by 0.1% after the end of each yearly period.

3. A salesperson receives commission of 10% of his/hers annual sales up to £20,000 and an additional 1% per £1,000 for amounts over £20,000. The maximum percentage commission allowable is however limited to 15%.

   Write a program to calculate the total commission received for annual sales of £19,750, £47,500 and £73,250.

4. Write a program that reads in the examination number of candidates together with the percentage marks attained in a given examination. The marks have to be graded as follows:

   Over 70%, A; 60 – 69%, B; 50 – 59%, C; 40 – 49%, D; Below 40%, F.

   The program should print, under suitable headings, the candidate number, mark and grade for each candidate. Arrange for the program to stop when a negative candidate number is entered.

5. Write a program to compute the following expression:

$$Y = \begin{cases} 1 + (1 - x^2) & \text{if } x \le 0 \\ 1 - (1 + x^2) & \text{if } x > 0 \end{cases}$$

   Use the DO loop to create values for the variable x from -3 to $+3$ in steps of 0.2.

   Print x and Y for each iteration of the loop, under appropriate headings.

4. SUBPROGRAMS

Standard arithmetic functions

Fortran contains functions to perform many mathematical operations. They relieve the user from programming his own small routines to calculate such common functions as logarithms, square roots, sines of angles, and so on. Fortran's mathematical functions have a call name followed by a parenthesized argument. They are pre-defined and may be used anywhere in a program. Some of Fortran's most common standard functions are listed below.

Standard Fortran Functions

Call Name	Meaning	Mode of argument
ABS(X)	Absolute value of X	Real
ACOS(X)	Arc-cosine of X	Real
AINT(X)	Truncation of X, returns a real value	Real
ALOG(X)	Natural logarithm of X	Real
ALOG10(X)	Logarithm to base 10 of X	Real
ASIN(X)	Arc-sine of X	Real
ATAN(X)	Arc-tangent of X	Real
COS(X)	Cosine of angle X, (X is in radians)	Real
COSH(X)	Hyperbolic cosine of X	Real
EXP(A)	Raises e to the power of X	Either
FLOAT(N)	Convert N to a real	Integer
IABS(N)	Absolute value of X	Integer
IFIX(X)	Convert X to an integer	Real
INT(X)	Truncation of X, returns an integer value	Real
SIN(X)	Sine of angle X, (X is in radians)	Real
SINH(X)	Hyperbolic sine	Real
SIGN(N,X)	Sign of X − +N if positive − N if negative	Same as arguments
SQRT(A)	Returns the square root of A	Either
TAN(X)	Tangent of angle X, (X is in radians)	Real
TANH(X)	Hyperbolic tangent	Real

Function calls can be used as expressions or elements of expressions wherever expressions are legal. The argument X, A or N of the function can be a constant, a variable, an expression or another function. A further explanation of the use of these functions is given below.

SIN(X), COS(X) and TAN(X)
The sine, cosine and tangent functions require an argument angle expressed in radians. If the angle is stated in degrees, conversion to radians can be achieved with the relation RADIANS = DEGREES*PI/180.0, where PI = 3.141592654.

ASIN(X), ACOS(X) and ATAN(X)
The arc-sine, arc-cosine and arc-tangent functions return a value in radians, in the range +1.570796 to -1.570796 corresponding to the value of a sine, cosine or tangent supplied as the argument X. Conversion to degrees is achieved with the relation DEGREES = RADIANS*180.0/PI, where PI = 3.141592654.

SQRT(X)
The SQRT() function returns the square root of the number supplied to it.

We shall illustrate the use of the above functions by considering a simple problem involving a 2 m long ladder resting against a wall. We assume that the angle between ladder and ground is 60 degrees and with the help of simple trigonometry we shall work out the vertical distance between the top of the ladder and the ground, the horizontal distance between the foot of the ladder and the wall and also the ratio of the vertical to horizontal distance.

The program uses the trigonometric functions SIN(), COS(), TAN(), ATAN() and also the function SQRT() to solve the problem. In addition, it calculates the original angle and ladder length.

Note: As Fortran 77 can accept variable names written in lower case, we use this in the program following. The choice of capitalizing the first letter of each variable name is purely personal preference. However, the length of such variable is still restricted to six characters.

```
              1        2        3      · 4
12345678901234567890123456789012345678901234567890
C LADDER AGAINST WALL
      REAL Length
      Angle=60
      PI=3.141592654
      Arads=Angle*PI/180.0
      Vert=2*SIN(Arads)
      Horiz=2*COS(Arads)
      Ratio=TAN(Arads)
      PRINT *,'ORIG ANGLE=',Angle
      PRINT *,'VERT DIST=',Vert
      PRINT *,'HORIZ DIST=',Horiz
      PRINT *,'RATIO=',Ratio
      Arads2=ATAN(Vert/Horiz)
      Angle2=Arads2*180.0/PI
      PRINT *,'CALC ANGLE=',Angle2
      Length=SQRT(Vert**2 + Horiz**2)
      PRINT *,'CALC LADDER LENGTH=',Length
      STOP
      END
```

On executing the program, Fortran will respond with

```
ORIG ANGLE=  60.000000
VERT DIST=   1.732051
HORIZ DIST=  9.999999E-01
RATIO=       1.732051
CALC ANGLE=  60.000000
CALC LADDER LENGTH=    2.000000
```

EXP(X)
The exponential function raises the number e to the power of X. The EXP() function is the inverse of the ALOG() function. The relation is

    ALOG(EXP(X)) = X

ALOG(X) and ALOG10(X)
The logarithms to base e and base 10 are given by these functions. Antilogarithm functions are not given but they can easily be derived using the following identities:

    Antilog(X) = e**X   (base e. This is EXP(X))
    Antilog(X) = 10**X   (base 10)

45

ABS(X)

The ABS() function returns the absolute (that is, positive) value of a given number. For example ABS(1.234) is 1.234, while ABS(-2.345) is returned as 2.345.

The ABS() function can be used to detect whether the values of two variables say, X and Y, are within an acceptable limit by using the statement in the form

```
IF (ABS(X-Y) .LT. 0.0001) THEN
```

in which case the block of statements following the THEN will be executed only if the absolute difference of the two variables is less than the specified limit, indicating that they are approximately equal. We need to use the ABS() function in the above statement otherwise a negative difference, no matter how small, would be less than the specified small positive number.

——————————— **Problem 4.1** ———————————

Newton's method of finding the square root of a number x is as follows:

(a) Make a guess at the square root, say q. A good approximation for this could be build into the program as $q = x/2$.

(b) Find $r = x/q$

(c) Find the average of r and q

(d) If r is approximately equal to q (use the absolute function in the statement IF (ABS(r-q) .LT. 0.001), then the average in (c) gives a good approximation of the square root

(e) Otherwise, take the average as the new value of q and repeat from (b).

Write a program capable of finding the square root of any number.

INT(X) and AINT(X)

The integer function returns the value of X rounded down to the nearest integer. Thus, INT(6.97) returns the value 6, whilst INT(-6.789) returns the value -7.

Numbers can be rounded to the nearest whole number, rather than rounding down, by using the function INT(X + 0.5). For example, INT(5.67 + 0.5) returns the value 6. It can also be used to round to any given number of decimal places, by the following expression:

```
AINT(X*10**D+0.5)/10**D
```

where D is a positive integer supplied by the user. For rounding to the first decimal, D = 1; to the fifth decimal, D = 5. The program given below illustrates this point.

```
          1         2         3         4
12345678901234567890123456789012345678901234567890
C ROUNDING NUMBERS
      INTEGER D
10    PRINT *,'ENTER A NUMBER '
      READ *,X
      IF (X .GT. 0.0) THEN
        PRINT *,'HOW MANY DEC PLACES? '
        READ *,D
        Y=AINT(X*10**D+0.5)/10**D
        PRINT *,Y
        GOTO 10
      ENDIF
      STOP
      END
```

Type the program and execute it. Results of a typical execution are given below.

```
ENTER A NUMBER
1.23456
HOW MANY DEC PLACES?
3
1.235000

ENTER A NUMBER
25.6789
HOW MANY DEC PLACES?
2
25.680000
```

To stop the program enter a number less than 1.

User-defined functions

In some programs it may be necessary to use the same mathematical expression in several places, often using different data. Fortran user-defined functions enable definition of unique operations or expressions. These can then be called in the same manner as standard functions.

The user-defined function is identified by a call name followed by a parenthesized argument. Such a function however, must be defined using the FUNCTION statement which, in general, is placed at the end of the main program, that is, after the END statement. The following program which calculated the volume of a cylinder, illustrates the use of a user-defined function.

```
          1         2         3         4         5
12345678901234567890123456789012345678901234567890
C USER-DEFINED FUNCTION - VOLUME OF A CYLINDER
        PRINT *,'RADIUS OF CYLINDER?'
        READ *,Radius
        PRINT *,'HEIGHT OF CYLINDER?'
        READ *,Height
        PRINT *,'VOLUME=',Volume(Radius,Height)
        STOP
        END
        FUNCTION Volume(R,H)
        PI=3.141592654
        Base=PI*R**2
        Vol=Base*H
        RETURN
        END
```

The function is defined at the end of the main program and two parameters are passed to it. Radius and Height are the actual arguments and the numbers held in them are passed to the two formal arguments R and H. There must be the same number of actual arguments in the call statement as there are formal arguments in the subprogram definition, as there is a one to one correspondence between these two parameters. If the first actual argument is real, then the first formal argument must also be real.

Note that the result of the calculation is RETURNed to the main program through the function name (Volume, in this case), therefore the user must bare in mind that the first letter of the function's call name indicates whether a real or an integer value is returned.

48

Subprograms such as the user-defined function discussed above, or the subroutines to be discussed shortly, are self-contained program units which can perform specific functions. Furtheremore, all parameters, variables and labels within the subprogram are local and have no connection with similar quantities in the main program. Declaration of integer or real variables with the INTEGER or REAL statements can be made on the line following the FUNCTION statement. This makes it possible to build up a library of standard subprograms, which can then be used as building blocks to assemble new, lengthier programs.

──────────────── **Problem 4.2** ────────────────
Modify the program given above so that it incorporates a second user-defined function which rounds, to the second decimal place, the calculated values for the volumes. Use the formula given under the AINT() function with a value for D = 2. Remember to declare D as an integer variable.

──────────────────────────────────

Subroutines
Subroutines are in many ways similar to user-defined functions. However, the major difference between them is that, whereas functions return a value to the main program, subroutines can be used to write information on the screen, the printer or the disc, as well as carry out complicated calculations which can be passed to the main program through parameters in the argument list.

Thus, a subroutine is a section of a program which is given a name and which can be called by name from any part of the program. After the subroutine has been executed, program control is returned to the statement following the calling statement. The general form of a subroutine which could be used to, say, calculate the sum of money returned on an investment, is written as follows:

```
SUBROUTINE Invest(Princ,Rate,Years)
        !
        !
        !
RETURN
END
```

To call this subroutine from any part of the program, we must use the following call statement

```
CALL Invest(A,B,C)
```

where variables A, B and C are the actual arguments. All the rules relating to parameter passing, as well as local variables and labels (discussed in the user-defined function section) are applicable to subroutines.

Fig. 4.1 shows in diagrammatic form an example of the flow of a program when a subroutine is incorporated. When Fortran encounters the call statement CALL X in the main body of the program, it branches to the first statement of the subroutine SUB-ROUTINE X, and continues to execute the statements within the subprogram until the RETURN statement is encountered. RETURN diverts the program flow to the statement immediately following the call statement.

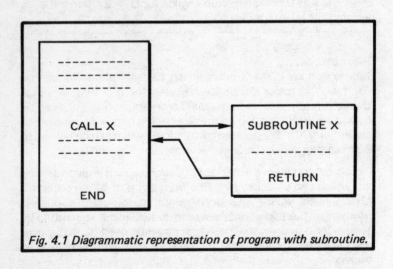

Fig. 4.1 Diagrammatic representation of program with subroutine.

Successive call statements can branch to the same subroutine. Each time the RETURN statement is reached, the main program is resumed at the last call statement from which it branched.

The following program, which calculates the compound interest on money lent, will be used to illustrate the use of subroutines. The program calculates the compound interest using the formula

Amount = Princ*(1.0 + Rate/100.0)**Years

where Princ (abbreviated for Principal) is the money lent, and Amount is what it amounts to in time Years at Rate per cent per annum.

```
            1         2         3         4         5
   1234567890123456789012345678901234567890123456789 0
   C COMPOUND INTEREST
         INTEGER Y
         REAL Inter
         PRINT *,'AMOUNT LENT?'
         READ *,P
         PRINT *,'INTEREST RATE?'
         READ *,R
         PRINT *,'NUMBER OF YEARS?'
         READ *,N
         PRINT 10
   10    FORMAT(//,1X,'YEARS',10X,'INTEREST'
         &,14X,'AMOUNT'/)
         DO 100 Y=1,N
         CALL Invest(P,R,Y,Amount)
         Inter=Amount-P
         PRINT 20,Y,Inter,Amount
   20    FORMAT(1X,I3,2F20.2)
   100   CONTINUE
         STOP
         END
   C CALCULATE COMPOUND INTEREST
         SUBROUTINE Invest(Princ,Rate,Years,Amount)
         INTEGER Years
         Amount=Princ*(1.0+Rate/100.0)**Years
         RETURN
         END
```

After entering the investment parameters P, R and N, the subroutine Invest is called several times from within the DO-100 loop. The parameters are passed to it at the same time through the argument list of the call statement. The values of these parameters are then used as the variables Princ, Rate and Years in the subroutine. After executing all the statements within the subroutine, program control passes back to the statement following the CALL in the main program where the value of Inter (short for Interest) is calculated prior to PRINTing the results.

Note that Amount, the result of the numerical calculation within the subroutine, is passed back to the main program via the parameter list. So, in a subroutine the parameter list is used to pass numeric values from the main program to the subprogram as well as passing results (there could be more than one) back to the main program.

The actual name of the subroutine (unlike that of a function) has nothing to do with numeric values, and as such can be called by any name we choose, provided it is less than six characters long.

Type this program into your computer and execute it using the values of 5000, 11 and 15 for P, R and N respectively. A program output using these numbers is given below.

```
AMOUNT LENT?
5000
INTEREST RATE?
11
NUMBER OF YEARS?
15
```

YEARS	INTEREST	AMOUNT
1	550.00	5550.00
2	1160.50	6160.50
3	1838.15	6838.15
4	2590.35	7590.35
5	3425.29	8425.29
6	4352.07	9352.07
7	5380.80	10380.80
8	6522.69	11522.69
9	7790.18	12790.18
10	9197.10	14197.10
11	10758.79	15758.79
12	12492.25	17492.25
13	14416.40	19416.40
14	16552.20	21552.20
15	18922.95	23922.95

The DATA statement in program segments
It is often convenient to initialize values of constants in a program segment. This can be achieved by the use of the DATA statement which takes the following form:

DATA $k_1/d_1/$, $k_2/d_2/$, ... $k_j/d_j/$

where k_j is a list of constant names and d_j is a list of numerical values. Each of these numerical values may be preceded by n, where n is an unsigned integer and indicates that the numerical value is to be specified n times.

For example, the statement

```
DATA A,B,C/3*0.0/
```

initializes to zero the three constant names A, B and C.

There must be a one-to-one correspondence between the list of constant names and the numerical values. Except in the case of a string constant (to be discussed in detail in the next chapter), the item name and its corresponding value must be of the same mode. For string constants, their name should be declared in an INTEGER statement and must be large enough to contain the assigned character(s).

The following two statements have the same effect.

```
DATA A/3.55/, B/6.45/, K/3/
DATA A, B, K/3.55, 6.45, 3/
```

The following two statements may be used to assign strings to the constant names ASTER, DOT and BLANK, which may be required in a graphing program.

```
CHARACTER ASTER, DOT, BLANK
DATA ASTER, DOT, BLANK/'*', '.', ' '/
```

The DATA statement is not executable, which means that the assignment of values to constant names does not take place during the execution of the program. Instead, the values assigned by it, are placed in memory when the program is first compiled. For this very reason, the DATA statement must appear at the beginning of a program segment (main program or either type of subprogram) prior to any other executable statement.

Although it is legal to redefine the values of constant names after initialization, it is best avoided as should they be redefined in a program then it becomes impossible to re-initialize them through the DATA statement again — which will be the case if the DATA statement appears in a subprogram which is repeatedly called from the main program.

The initialization of constant names with the use of the DATA statement is not allowed if these constant names have been declared in a blank COMMON statement (to be discussed shortly). In order to enter data into a labelled COMMON (see next section) it is necessary to do so through a subprogram called BLOCK DATA (also be discussed shortly).

COMMON and EQUIVALENCE in program segments

The blank COMMON statement:

It has been stated earlier that each subprogram has its own variable names; the names X and Y in the main program are not necessarily taken to be the same as the names X and Y in the subprogram. If we wish them to be the same, we write

```
COMMON X, Y
```

in both the main program and the subprogram. The compiler
assigns both sets of variables to the same location in memory.

The statement is not limited to this kind of use only. We can write

```
COMMON A, K, B        (in the main program)
```

and

```
COMMON X, M, Y        (in the subprogram)
```

where A and X are assigned to the same location, as are K and M,
and B and Y. There must exist a one-to-one correspondence
between real and integer variables in the two COMMON
statements.

Thus, here is the flexibility of using someone else's subroutine
with a main program which does not even use the same variable
names; we make the connection with the COMMON statement.
The same flexibility can be applied to the calling arguments of a
subroutine. we can write:

```
CALL ASUB(A, B, K)           (in the main program)
```

and

```
SUBROUTINE ASUB(X, Y, M)      (in the subroutine)
```

Again, there must exist a one-to-one correspondence between
real and integer variables in the actual arguments of the CALL
statement and the dummy arguments of the subroutine.

Note: A variable name appearing in the COMMON statement,
must not appear in the argument list of a subprogram.

The labelled COMMON statement:

Another kind of COMMON statement exists which is called labelled COMMON, and is particularly useful if names in different subprograms and main program are to share the same location. The name of this common location, however, must not exist in any of the program segments.

As an example, consider a main program with a variable A and three subprograms with variables B, C and D respectively. All four variables can be made to share the same location by declaring

```
COMMON /X/A,B,C,D
```

where variable X does not exist in either the main program or the subprograms. Thus, whenever A, B, C or D are referenced, this will be a reference to the location called X.

The EQUIVALENCE statement:

The EQUIVALENCE statement causes two or more variables in one program (main program or subprogram) to be assigned to the same storage location. This differs from the COMMON statement which causes variables in different program segments to be assigned to the same storage location.

Thus, the EQUIVALENCE statement is useful in two different ways: (a) It allows the programmer who has used say X, Y and Z in one program to be assigned to the same storage location simply by writing

```
EQUIVALENCE (X,Y,Z)
```

(b) It allows the same storage location to be used by two or more variables, within a long program, which are different but are never needed at the same time. One EQUIVALENCE statement can establish equivalence between more than one set of variables. For example,

```
EQUIVALENCE (A,B,C), (X,Y)
```

will cause A, B and C to be assigned to one storage location, while X and Y are assigned to another.

Again, there must be a one-to-one correspondence between real and integer variables that are being made equivalent.

The BLOCK DATA statement

Data may never be entered into blank COMMON with a DATA statement. In order to enter data into labelled COMMON it is necessary to write a special subprogram called BLOCK DATA. The only statements which are allowed within a BLOCK DATA subprogram are DIMENSION, COMMON, EQUIVALENCE, REAL, INTEGER or other type declaration statements, the DATA statements and also the END statement which finishes the subprogram. For example,

```
BLOCK DATA
COMMON /X/A,B,C,D
DATA A,B,C,D/4*1.0/
END
```

will allow initialization of location called X to 1.0 and by inference will initialize A, B, C and D to the same value.

Functions as arguments — The EXTERNAL statement

It is permissible to use a function name as an argument in a subroutine. If this is done however, it is necessary to list the function name in an EXTERNAL statement in the main program to distinguish the function name from that of a variable.

Below is a main program which calls a subroutine named FUN written in terms of only one statement $Z = F(R)$, where F stands for the function to be evaluated according to the argument in the CALL statement.

```
EXTERNAL COS, SIN, Y
R=1.0
CALL FUN(R,COS,Z)
---
---
CALL FUN(R,SIN,Z)
---
---
CALL FUN (R,Y,Z)
---
---
END
```

and following the main program will be the subprograms:

```
SUBROUTINE FUN(R,F,Z)
Z=F(R)
RETURN
END

FUNCTION Y(R)
PI=3.141592654
Y=2.0*PI*R**2
RETURN
END
```

Here it is seen the SUBROUTINE FUN is first called to evaluate
$Z = COS(R)$, then is called to evaluate $Z = SIN(R)$ and finally to
evaluate $Z = Y(R)$, where Y is a FUNCTION subprogram.

———————————————— **Problem 4.3** ————————————————
Modify the solution to Problem 4.2 by making FUNCTION Volume
into a SUBROUTINE and declaring FUNCTION Round as an
EXTERNAL function so that it can be called from within the argument list of the CALL Volume statement. Use the variable Subst
within the SUBROUTINE argument list as a substitute for Round,
the FUNCTION name, and pass the result of the rounded value
back to the main program via the variable Rvalue.

Finally, use the DATA statement to give constant PI its numerical
value.

Exercises

1. Three truck sizes are available to move a given volume of earth. Write a program to calculate the number of truck loads of each size required, using the following logic.

   (a) The large trucks must be used first, if possible, as long as they are full

   (b) The medium size trucks should be used next, as long as they are full

   (c) The smallest trucks should take the remaining load, if any.

   The information to be processed by your program is as follows:

   (i)   Volume of ore to be moved,

   (ii) Capacity (in volume) of the largest truck,

   (iii) Capacity (in volume) of the middle-sized truck,

   (iv) Capacity (in volume) of the smallest truck.

   Your program should accept data consisting of these four values and with the use of the INT() function should evaluate the number of trucks required and produce the following tabulated output.

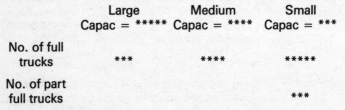

Volume of earth to be moved = ******

	Large Capac = *****	Medium Capac = ****	Small Capac = ***
No. of full trucks	***	****	*****
No. of part full trucks			***

Note that only small sized trucks could be part full.

2. Write a program which reads the coefficients A, B and C of a quadratic equation, i.e.

$$Ax^2 + Bx + C = 0$$

and uses the formula

$$x = \frac{-B \pm \sqrt{\{B^2 - 4AC\}}}{2A}$$

to solve for the two roots of the equation. The program must test whether $A = 0$, as well as whether $\{B^2 - 4AC\}$ is equal, greater or less than zero. If $\{B^2 - 4AC\}$ is negative, then the two roots of the equation are deemed to be complex in which case the real $(-B/2A)$ and imaginary $(\pm\{B^2 - 4AC\}/2A)$ parts of each root must be given separately.

Test your program with the following data:

A	B	C
1	-10	25
0	-2	1
0.02	-0.04	0.02
1	2	5
1	0	-1
1	0	1
1	2	1

3. Two points A and B have coordinates given by (x_1, y_1) and (x_2, y_2) respectively. Write a program to calculate the distance of separation between the points given by

$$\sqrt{\{(y_2-y_1)^2 + (x_2-x_1)^2\}}$$

However, instead of using the internal function SQRT(), use the program given as the solution to Problem 4.1, suitably adapted to a function subprogram to evaluate the square root.

4. In Fortran there are only three major differences between a FUNCTION and a SUBROUTINE. One of these differences has to do with the manner each subprogram is called, while the other two have to do with the way parameters are passed between the subprogram and the main program. Explain fully.

5. Re-write the solution to Problem 3.2 suitably modified as a subroutine with the three parameters A, B and C in its argument list. Then write a main program that reads the lengths of the three sides of a triangle and calls the subroutine to sort their values in ascending order so that variable C holds the largest of the three. Then use the identity

$C^2 = A^2 + B^2$

to test whether the three sides form a right triangle or not.

For non-integer values for A, B and C you will find that it is necessary to use the ABS() function in order to test whether $A^2 + B^2$ is approximately equal to C^2.

5. STRINGS AND ARRAYS

Character constants

A sequence of characters is referred to as a literal, and a literal in single quotation marks is called a string. For example,

ABC12 is a literal, and 'ABC12' is a string.

Just as numerical values can be assigned to variables and constants, strings can be assigned to character constants, provided they have been declared in a CHARACTER statement. The CHARACTER declaration statement must give information on the length of the string and takes the following form:

```
CHARACTER A, B*5, C*20
```

where A is deemed to be one character long, while B and C are 5 characters and 20 characters long respectively. The program below assigns a string to character constant B, READs from the keyboard a character and assigns it to character constant A, performs a logical comparison and depending on the outcome it 'concatenates' the contents of B to the string ' YOU TYPED ' – note the spaces in the string – and the contents of A by using the concatenation operator //.

```
          1         2         3         4         5
12345678901234567890123456789012345678901234567890
C CHARACTER CONSTANTS AND CONCATENATION
      CHARACTER A,B*5,C*20
      B='HELLO'
      PRINT *,'Please enter Y or press any other key'
      READ 10, A
10    FORMAT(A1)
      IF (A .EQ. 'Y') THEN
        C=B//' YOU TYPED '//A
      ELSE
        C=' YOU TYPED '//A
      END IF
      PRINT *, C
      STOP
      END
```

On executing the program Fortran writes

```
HELLO YOU TYPED Y
```

if you pressed the letter Y, otherwise it writes

```
YOU TYPED #
```

where # stands for the key pressed. Note that character comparison is case sensitive. Thus, responding with 'y' instead of 'Y' will give different results.

Note the form of the FORMAT statement associated with the READ statement which will also be valid in the case of a PRINT statement associated with character constant. It is known as the A Format (A stands for Alphanumeric) and takes the form

```
Aw
```

where w specifies the width of the input or output field, i.e. the number of characters associated with the specified character constant.

Fortran assigns a numeric code to each character on the keyboard, according to the ASCII code, as shown in Table 5.1. Thus, each letter of the alphabet is assigned a numeric value and as a result the letter A has a smaller value than B, letter B smaller than C, and so on.

When character constants and strings appear in an IF statement they are compared character by character from left to right on the basis of the ASCII values until a difference is found. If a character in that position in character constant A has the same ASCII code in the same position in string 'Y' (refer to the IF statement in the previous program), then A is equal to the string 'Y'. If all the characters in the same positions are identical but one string has more characters than the other, the longer string is the greater of the two. Thus, alphabetic strings can be placed easily in alphabetical order.

In the statements given so far, the character constants are considered in their entirety. Later on, however, we discuss a method whereby we can access any character within a given string to form a substring which can then be printed out or concatenated to other substrings or strings. This will allow complete string manipulation.

TABLE 5.1 ASCII Conversion Codes

Char	Abbr	Dec	Char	Abbr	Dec	Char	Abbr	Dec
CTRL @	nul	0	CTRL K	vt	11	CTRL V	syn	22
CTRL A	soh	1	CTRL L	ff	12	CTRL W	etb	23
CTRL B	stx	2	CTRL M	cr	13	CTRL X	can	24
CTRL C	etx	3	CTRL N	so	14	CTRL Y	em	25
CTRL D	eot	4	CTRL O	si	15	CTRL Z	sub	25
CTRL E	enq	5	CTRL P	dle	16	CTRL [	esc	27
CTRL F	ack	6	CTRL Q	dc1	17	CTRL \	fs	28
CTRL G	bel	7	CTRL R	dc2	18	CTRL]	gs	29
CTRL H	bs	8	CTRL S	dc3	19	CTRL ^	rs	30
CTRL I	ht	9	CTRL T	dc4	20	CTRL __	us	31
CTRL J	lf	10	CTRL U	nak	21			

Char	Dec	Char	Dec	Char	Dec
SPACE	32	@	64	'	96
!	33	A	65	a	97
"	34	B	66	b	98
.	35	C	67	c	99
$	36	D	68	d	100
%	37	E	69	e	101
&	38	F	70	f	102
'	39	G	71	g	103
(	40	H	72	h	104
)	41	I	73	i	105
*	42	J	74	j	106
+	43	K	75	k	107
,	44	L	76	l	108
–	45	M	77	m	109
.	46	N	78	n	110
/	47	O	79	o	111
0	48	P	80	p	112
1	49	Q	81	q	113
2	50	R	82	r	114
3	51	S	83	s	115
4	52	T	84	t	116
5	53	U	85	u	117
6	54	V	86	v	118
7	55	W	87	w	119
8	56	X	88	x	120
9	57	Y	89	y	121
:	58	Z	90	z	122
;	59	[	91	{	123
<	60	\	92			124
=	61	]	93	}	125
>	62	^	94	~	126
?	63	__	95	del	127

Note: In the table, groups of two or three lower case letters are abbreviations for standard ASCII control characters. Codes within the range 128 to 255 form the extended IBM character set. This can be accessed by typing a number within the range 128 to 255 on the numeric key pad while holding down the 'Alt' key. On releasing the Alt key the character represented by the typed decimal will appear on the screen.

String arrays

A number of strings can be stored under a common name in what is known as a string array. Let us assume that we have four names i.e. SMITH, JONES, BROWN and WILSON which we would like to store in a string array. In Fortran, whenever an array is to be used in a program, you must declare your intention to do so in a DIMENSION statement as shown in the program below, which allows you to read and store the four names into the common variable Name().

```
          1         2         3         4         5
12345678901234567890123456789012345678901234567890
C USE OF A STRING ARRAY
      CHARACTER*6 NAME(4)
      PRINT *,'ENTER FOUR NAMES'
      DO 100 I=1,4
        PRINT *,'ENTER NAME NO.',I
        READ 10, NAME(I)
   10   FORMAT(A6)
  100 CONTINUE
      STOP
      END
```

On executing this program type in the four names in the order given below

```
SMITH
JONES
BROWN
WILSON
```

A simple way to visualize a string array is as follows:

SMITH	JONES	BROWN	WILSON

The four names are stored in a common box which has four compartments, each compartment containing one name. Thus, NAME(2) refers to the 2nd compartment of string array NAME(), and NAME(4) to the 4th compartment. The CHARACTER statement tells Fortran that a string array called NAME() is to be used with maximum dimensions as given within the brackets following the array name (in this case 4). The length of each string within the array has been declared to be equal to 6 (the number following the asterisk after the CHARACTER statement). Finally, any reference to an array name within a program must be of the form

    NAME(I)

where I has a value between 1 and the maximum number given in the CHARACTER statement. Reference to NAME alone does not refer to the array and causes a compiling error to occur.

The following program will READ the name, location and telephone extension of five employees. Note that the data have been structured so that the commas separating the names from the locations and the locations from the telephone extensions have the same position within each string. This is achieved by adding spaces to compensate for different lengths of names etc. We do this at this stage in order to allow manipulation of these strings later. In the example, two DO loops are used to show that once data have been READ, they are stored in memory (unless overwritten). One loop would normally be sufficient.

```
          1         2         3         4         5
12345678901234567890123456789012345678901234567890
C USING A STRING ARRAY FOR EMPLOYEES
        CHARACTER*25 Employ(5)
        DO 100 I=1,5
          READ 10,Employ(I)
  10      FORMAT(A25)
 100    CONTINUE
        DO 200 I=1,5
          PRINT *,Employ(I)
 200    CONTINUE
        STOP
        END
```

Type this program into your computer under the name EMPLOY and compile it. The data we have to supply to it follows.

```
WILSON M.  ,ROOM 1.24, 395
SMITH M.   ,ROOM 2.6 ,7315
JONES B.M.,ROOM 6.19,1698
SMITH A.A.,ROOM 2.12, 456
BROWN C.   ,ROOM 3.1 , 432
```

Were we to execute the program and then supply it with the above data, Fortran would write the literals on the screen as they appear above. However, typing the above data every time we execute the program is a laborious task, as well as running the risk of making mistakes. A better method would be to type the data once into a data file and then READ the information from the file every time we needed to do so.

Data files in Fortran
To create a Fortran data file, use your editor and type the above information starting from column 1, as follows:

```
        1         2         3         4         5
1234567890123456789012345678901234567890123456789
WILSON M.  ,ROOM 1.24, 395
SMITH M.   ,ROOM 2.6 ,7315
JONES B.M.,ROOM 6.19,1698
SMITH A.A.,ROOM 2.12, 456
BROWN C.   ,ROOM 3.1 , 432
```

Save the file under the same filename as your Fortran source program, but give it the extension DAT (for DATA). The extension name might differ for different compilers, so check it with the staff of your computer department or the documentation supplied with your compiler. Once the data file has been created, your program looks for the correct extension during execution to READ data from it.

In MS-Fortran input can be taken in its entirety from a data file provided the information to use that data file is given in the execution command, as follows:

```
EMPLOY < EMPLOY.DAT
```

which tells Fortran to execute the file EMPLOY, but take input from the file EMPLOY.DAT. Indirection of I/O can be achieved with the general command

```
File < Infile > Outfile
```

66

where Infile is the data file that Fortran will READ for input information and Outfile is the data file to which output will be PRINTed. Either I/O data file can be omitted from the command.

Note that the above commands cause I/O to be read or printed in its entirety from/to the respective data file. If you need to read some data from a data file and then revert to keyboard input, then you must use the method discussed under section 'Substrings'.

On executing the program, Fortran READs the data file and PRINTs the output on the screen exactly as we typed it in. Do attempt this problem as we will return to it later when dealing with sorting techniques.

Substrings

We shall now introduce a method which allows substring creation and therefore string manipulation. For example, suppose we want to extract and print out only the names of the employees held in array Employ(). Fortran allows us to do this quite easily with the use of substring referencing. The statement

```
Employ(I)(1:10)
```

references the Ith string, but only from character 1 to character 10. Note that reference to the string array Employ has two bracket arguments; first is the Ith string of string array Employ() and second is the numerals 1:10 which refer to the number of characters of interest. Thus, using Employ(I)(1:1) will reference the first character of the Ith string, while using Employ(I)(25:25) references the last character of the Ith string.

As an example of the use of string arrays, consider the following program, which causes information on the quantity and price of several items in stock to be stored by Fortran. To extract information regarding details of items in stock, simply start the program and answer the questions posed.

Firstly, the program reads and stores into string array Item() the actual names of the items in stock, while at the same time their quantity and price are read into Stock(). In response to the question 'WHICH ITEM', the name of an item, associated with the string variable Name, is typed in. If it is END, then the program stops.

If, however, it has any other name, it causes a loop to be set up which compares in turn the contents of Item() with Name. If they are found to be equal, it prints the required information held in Stock(), otherwise it returns to the question WHICH ITEM?

Type in the program under the filename STOCK, paying particular attention to the spaces inserted within the various PRINT statements, and compile it.

```
             1         2         3         4.        5
1234567890123456789012345678901234567890123456789 0
C STOCKTAKING
      CHARACTER*16 Item(4), Name
      CHARACTER*8 Stock(4)
      OPEN(UNIT=5,FILE='STOCK.DAT')
      DO 100 I=1,4
        READ 10,Item(I),Stock(I)
  10    FORMAT(A16,1X,A8)
 100  CONTINUE
      CLOSE(UNIT=5)
  20  PRINT *,'WHICH ITEM?'
      READ 30, Name
  30  FORMAT(A16)
      IF (Name .NE. 'END') THEN
        DO 200 I=1,4
          IF (Item(I) .EQ. Name) THEN
            PRINT *,'>>>>>> ',Stock(I)(1:3),
     &        ' IN STOCK AT £',Stock(I)(5:8),' EACH'
          END IF
 200    CONTINUE
        GOTO 20
      END IF
      STOP
      END
```

The program requires a four line data file (see OPEN statement) called STOCK.DAT which holds the following information:

```
             1         2         3         4         5
1234567890123456789012345678901234567890123456789 0
INK ERASER        200 0.10
PENCIL ERASER     320 0.15
TYPING ERASER      25 0.25
CORRECTION FLUID  150 0.50
```

Note the spaces used to separate and line up the different parts of information.

On executing the program, Fortran OPENs a channel of communication via UNIT 5 to a FILE by the name STOCK.DAT (see statement prior to the beginning of the DO-100 loop), READs that file from within the DO-100 loop and then CLOSEs that UNIT with the statement following the end of the DO-100 loop. This is essential if further information is to be taken from the keyboard (the default *) input unit. Normally, all I/O units are automatically closed after execution of a program stops, but to divert control from unit 5 to the default * I/O unit while a program is in progress, the first unit must be CLOSEd. Alternatively, you could specify a different unit number (other than 5) for the input unit associated with a data file (say unit 3), so that both could remain activated (open for input) at the same time.

Here output and then input is diverted to the external unit * which represents the screen and keyboard for the correct execution of statements from label 20 onwards. Fortran now responds with the message

        WHICH ITEM?

and awaits your input from the keyboard. Below, we present a typical run of this program.

        WHICH ITEM? PENCIL

        WHICH ITEM? PENCIL ERASER

        >>>>>> 320 IN STOCK AT £0.15 EACH

        WHICH ITEM? CORRECTION FLUID

        >>>>>> 150 IN STOCK AT £0.50 EACH

        WHICH ITEM? END

which causes execution of the program to stop.

─────────────────────── **Problem 5.1** ───────────────────────
Modify the above stocktaking program so that you only need to enter the first three letters of each item whenever the question 'WHICH ITEM' is asked. The output of your program should, however, print the full name of each item.
───

Overlaying

Perhaps the most important use of string arrays is that of building up string overlays. What we mean by this is the ability to create an empty string array of fixed length and then place characters in it anywhere along its length, in any order we choose. The following program will help to illustrate this effect.

```
          1         2         3         4         5
 12345678901234567890123456789012345678901234567890
C OVERLAYING
       CHARACTER*1 Aster, Line(40)
       INTEGER Pos
       Aster='*'
       DO 100 I=1,40
       Line(I)=' '
  100  CONTINUE
       PRINT *,'How Many Stars?'
       READ *, N
       DO 200 I=1,N
   10  PRINT *,'Enter Position',I
       READ *,Pos
       IF (Pos .LT. 1 .OR. Pos .GT. 40) THEN
         PRINT *,'PLEASE RE-ENTER'
         GOTO 10
       ENDIF
       Line(Pos)=Aster
  200  CONTINUE
       PRINT *,
      &'          1         2         3         4'
       PRINT *,
      &'12345678901234567890123456789012345678901234567890'
       PRINT *,Line
       END
```

In the CHARACTER declaration we create a single character string Aster and a string array Line with 40 strings, each capable of holding a single character. We then assign an asterisk to the string Aster and fill the string array Line with blanks. Subsequently, we overlay a number of asterisks onto the blanked string array Line by specifying the position Pos in which we wish to place an asterisk. The result is then printed out under a 'line ruler' so that we can check the exact position of each asterisk.

On executing the program, Fortran will respond with a series of questions. Enter the numbers following the question marks.

70

```
How Many Stars?
3
Enter Position 1
35
Enter Position 2
24
Enter Position 3
12
```

which will cause the following output to be printed out:

```
         1         2         3         4
12345678901234567890123456789012345678901234567890
         *                  *        *
```

This overlaying technique can be used to present visually the results of an experiment in the form of a scatter plot or a crude graph.

─────────────── **Problem 5.2** ───────────────

Write a program which uses string manipulation to allow:

(a)   the printing of a given letter specified by entering a number within the range from 1 to 26, and

(b)   the printing of a number corresponding to the position of a given letter within the alphabet, by entering any given letter.

───

Subscripted numeric variables

Subscripted numeric variables permit the representation of many quantities with one variable name. A particular quantity is indicated by writing a subscript in parentheses after the variable name. Individual quantities are called elements, while a set of elements is called an array. A subscripted variable may have one, two or three subscripts, and it then represents a one- two- or three- dimensional array.

The elements of a one-dimensional array can be represented as follows:

A(1)   A(2)   A(3)   A(4)

while those of a two-dimensional array as:

```
A(1,1)   A(1,2)   A(1,3)   A(1,4)
A(2,1)   A(2,2)   A(2,3)   A(2,4)
A(3,1)   A(3,2)   A(3,3)   A(3,4)
```

The first of the two subscripts refers to the row number, running from 1 to the maximum number of declared rows, and the second subscript to the column number, running from 1 to the maximum number of declared columns.

A three-dimensional array can be thought of as stacked two-dimensional arrays with the third subscript, running from 1 to the maximum height of the stack.

In the computer, however, arrays are stored with elements following one another on a single line as shown below.

```
A(1,1)   A(2,1)   A(3,1)   A(1,2)   A(2,2)   A(3,2)
```

with the first subscript changing more rapidly than the second, and the second more rapidly than the third (in the case of a three-dimensional array). Provided that this is recognized and understood, we can use the previous pictorial form of representation for programming purposes.

Numerical arrays must be declared prior to their use in a DIMENSION statement which precedes any executable statements in a program, just as we had to declare strings in a CHARACTER statement. The form of the statement is shown below.

```
DIMENSION X(15), Y(3,5), Z(3,5,4)
```

where array X() has been declared to be a one-dimensional array with a maximum of 15 elements, array Y(,) has been declared as a two-dimensional array of 3 rows and 5 columns, and array Z(,,) as a three-dimensional array of 3 rows and 5 columns stacked 4 deep.

The following program illustrates the use of numerical arrays. Data are read into a one-dimensional array and subsequently the contents of the even numbered elements are summed into variable Even, while the contents of all the odd elements are summed into variable Odd.

```
              1            2          3           4          5
12345678901234567890123456789012345678901234567890
C NUMERICAL ARRAY
        DIMENSION Value(16)
C READ & STORE INTO Value() 16 NUMBERS
        PRINT *,'ENTER 16 NUMBERS'
        DO 100 I=1,16
          PRINT *,'No.',I
          READ *, Value(I)
  100   CONTINUE
C SUM EVEN ELEMENTS
        Even=0.0
        DO 200 I=2,16,2
          Even=Even+Value(I)
  200   CONTINUE
C SUM ODD ELEMENTS
        Odd=0.0
        DO 300 I=1,15,2
          Odd=Odd+Value(I)
  300   CONTINUE
C PRINT CONTENTS OF ARRAY
        DO 400 I=1,16
          PRINT *, Value(I)
  400   CONTINUE
        PRINT *,'EVEN=',Even,'ODD=',Odd
```

On executing this program, and entering the following 16 reques-
ted numbers

   7,6,1,9,7,14,39,24,19,32,21,8,5,15,28,4

the contents of array Value(), are PRINTed out one under the
other. Under these the output

   EVEN=112 ODD=127

appears on the screen.

Note. Had we used the previous program to store more than 20
numbers and then attempted to print them on the screen in a vertical format, we would lose the beginning of the printout as the
screen scrolled upwards. To halt program execution temporarily,
press

   'CTRL'S

To restart program execution from the point of interruption, press
'CTRL'S again. Try this command by modifying the previous program so that it READs, stores and PRINTs 50 numbers.

73

Modify the program solution to Problem 5.1 so that the numerical parts of the data are stored in array Stock(,), which has been appropriately declared as a two-dimensional array.

───

Reading and Printing in array form

A vertical one-dimensional array can be read in from an appropriately structured data file or printed out simply using the DO loop. For example,

```
      DO 100 I=1,8
        READ 10, A(I)
100   CONTINUE
 10     FORMAT(F10.3)
```

executes the READ statement 8 times, each time referencing the FORMAT statement.

If, however, we require to print such an array on one line, or to read data placed in a one-line data file, we must use the 'implied DO loop' statement, as follows:

```
      PRINT 10, (A(J), J=1,8)
 10   FORMAT(8F10.3)
```

The FORMAT statement is only scanned once and therefore we must supply information regarding all 8 numbers at once. Note the form of the implied DO loop. As the instructions within the brackets are executed first, reference is made to all 8 elements of A(J), while the actual PRINT is executed only once with the result that all 8 elements of the array are printed horizontally on the same line.

Finally, a two-dimensional array of I rows and J columns can be read in or printed out by a combination of both the DO loop (to read/print each row) and the implied DO loop (to read/print the columns). For example, the program segment

```
      DO 100 I=1,30
        PRINT 10, (A(I,J), J=1,8)
100   CONTINUE
 10 FORMAT(8F10.3)
```

will cause Fortran to PRINT 8 floating point numbers (each in a field of 10) on the same line, and repeat this 30 times. Alternatively, the implied DO loop may be used alone to print out an array of 10 columns by 8 rows by adopting the following statements:

```
      PRINT 10, ((X(I,J), J=1,10, I=1,8)
10    FORMAT(8(10F8.3)/))
```

The innermost bracket of the FORMAT statement will be executed first, allowing 10 fields to be printed before encountering the slash which will cause the next set of data to be printed on the next line. This is repeated 8 times. Within the implied DO loop, the 'innermost' control variable J varies faster. This is repeated 8 times.

Concatenation and the LEN() function

As we saw at the beginning of this chapter, Fortran allows the concatenation (joining together) of strings. This, together with the use of the LEN() function which simply returns the length of the string in its argument, allows more sophisticated manipulation of strings. We shall illustrate this by considering the following program in which the computer asks you to enter your first name first followed by your surname. It then concatenates the two with a space between them and prints the result which is held in string variable Name.

```
          1         2         3         4         5
123456789012345678901234567890123456789012345678901234567890
      CHARACTER Fname*20, Sname*20, Name*23
      PRINT *,'ENTER YOUR FIRST NAME PLEASE'
      READ 10, Fname
10    FORMAT(A)
      CALL HOWMANY(Fname,Lf)
      PRINT *,'ENTER YOUR SURNAME PLEASE'
      READ 10, Sname
      CALL HOWMANY(Sname,Ls)
      L=Lf+Ls+1
      IF (L .GT. 23) THEN
        Name=Fname(1:1)//'. '//Sname(1:Ls)
        L=Ls+3
      ELSE
        Name=Fname(1:Lf)//' '//Sname(1:Ls)
      ENDIF
      PRINT 20, Name
20    FORMAT(1X,A)
      END
```

75

```
                SUBROUTINE HOWMANY(Name,N)
                CHARACTER Name*24, SPACE
                SPACE=' '
                N=0
                DO 100 J=1,LEN(Name)
                IF (Name(J:J) .GT. SPACE) N=N+1
        100     CONTINUE
                RETURN
                END
```

Note that the function LEN() returns the declared length of the string constant contained in its argument. This is employed in SUBROUTINE HOWMANY, which had to be written in order to count the number of characters typed in response to the request for your first name and surname.

As it stands, the program is comparatively easy. However, using the overlaying techniques discussed earlier in the chapter, together with the use of the implied DO loop in a PRINT statement, can result in a somewhat more spectacular result. To illustrate this, add the following line to the main program prior to the END statement:

```
                CALL BOXIT(Name,L)
```

adding the following subroutine at the end of the program.

```
                SUBROUTINE BOXIT(Name,L)
                CHARACTER Name*24
                CHARACTER*1 BOX(27,27)
                DO 100 I=1,27
                  DO 100 J=1,27
                    BOX(I,J)=' '
        100     CONTINUE
                DO 300 I=1,L
                  IF (I .EQ. 1 .OR. I .EQ. L) THEN
                    DO 200 J=3,L+2
                      BOX(I,J)=Name(J-2:J-2)
        200       CONTINUE
                ENDIF
                BOX(I,1)=Name(I:I)
                BOX(I,L+4)=Name(I:I)
        300     CONTINUE
                DO 400 I=1,L
                  PRINT 10, (BOX(I,J), J=1,L+4)
         10     FORMAT(31X,27A1)
        400     CONTINUE
                RETURN
                END
```

Execute the program and supply it with your first name and surname. What you will see on the screen, if your name was John Brown, would be:

```
J John Brown J
o            o
h            h
n            n

B            B
r            r
o            o
w            w
n John Brown n
```

Note that the program has worked out the length of your full name and allowed enough space between the two vertical columns to write it horizontally on the first and last rows. Now re-execute the program, but this time type in a really long name, say CHRISTO-PHER VERYLONGFELLOW. Can you work out from the program lines and the output on your screen what has happened? Try it.

Exercises

1. The Fibonacci sequence starts with the numbers 1 and 1. The next number is the sum of these and subsequent numbers are the sum of the preceding pair. So we get:

   1, 1, 2, 3, 5, 8, 13, 21, ...

   Write a program to calculate the first 30 Fibonacci numbers and store them in an appropriate one-dimensional array. In a second one-dimensional array store the average of adjacent numbers. The printout should be headed appropriately.

2. Write a program employing a two-dimensional array to store the following data which are to be found in a data file.

   ```
             1         2         3         4         5
   12345678901234567890123456789012345678901234567890
      5.1   4.5   6.2   3.2   7.5   2.2   1.1
     15.0  13.0  12.7  18.6  21.4  12.5  20.5
   ```

   Output the data:

   (a) in the same FORMAT as that used to read the data in, and

   (b) in two vertical columns, the first array column appearing between the 9th and 11th printer position, and the second column appearing between the 19th and 22nd printer position.

3. A firm employing 8 persons allows travelling expenses based on the engine capacity of their cars as follows:

   > Up to 1199 cc, 15p per mile;
   > 1200-1499 cc, 19p per mile;
   > over 1500 cc, 23p per mile.

   Write a program to read from a data file for each employee, their name, car make, engine capacity of car, and distance travelled each month. The output should appear in tabular form, giving the above information and travelling expenses due.

4. A geologist is working with several hundred rock samples which fall into 20 classifications numbered from 1 to 20. Part of the experiment requires recording the weight of each rock sample and producing a table showing the average weight of each classification.

Assume that data are contained in a data file and are structured on N number of lines (N ≤ 1000), each line containing a classification number in column 1-2 and a weight in grams in columns 3-15, as shown below:

```
              1                 2
     12345678901234567890
     15          38.5
     11         155.1
     13          57.8
     20         199.3
      1          45.9
      .            .
      .            .
      .           ..
```

Write a program to read the information from the data file, counting the number in each classification and adding up their respective weights, by employing a 20-row by 4-column array with the first column containing the 'classification number', while columns two and three are used for the accumulation of 'numbers in each classification' and 'total weights', as shown below. For example, for classification number 15 which occurs only once in the data, the output would be as follows:

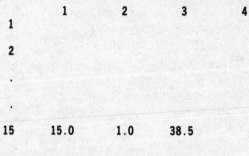

```
              1         2         3         4
     1

     2

     .

     .

    15       15.0      1.0      38.5

     .

     .

    20
```

79

Once the data file has been read and the data processed in the way suggested above, calculate and store the average weight of each classification in the fourth column of the array. Finally, arrange for the information held in the array to be printed out, in matrix form, under suitable headings.

5. Write a program to calculate the mean and standard deviation of a set of readings. Use the DO loop to read in each quantity x and store it in the first column of an array.

Calculate the running sum of x, the square of x, and the running sum of x^2, storing the results in the second, third and fourth column of the array, respectively.

Print in tabular form, under appropriate headings, the quantities x, Σx, x^2 and Σx^2. Then, calculate and print the values of the mean and standard deviation from

$$\text{Mean} = \frac{\Sigma x}{n} \qquad \text{S.D.} = \sqrt{\frac{\{n\Sigma x^2 - (\Sigma x)^2\}}{\{n(n-1)\}}}$$

where n is the total number of data entries.

6. NUMERICAL METHODS

In this chapter we shall use examples from mathematics, science and management to illustrate numerical methods for which Fortran is the ideal computer language. Naturally, it will help if the reader has some understanding of the relevant subject areas as we shall mainly concentrate on the method of solution rather than the derivation of equations.

Interpolation and extrapolation

Given the coordinates of two points A and B in an x-y system (see Fig. 6.1), we can interpolate (that is, find the coordinates of points lying between the two points A and B), or extrapolate (find the coordinates of points lying outside the given points) provided some assumption is made on the shape of the curve joining the two points.

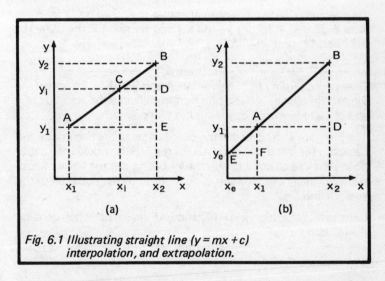

Fig. 6.1 Illustrating straight line ($y = mx + c$)
    interpolation, and extrapolation.

The program below makes the assumption that the two points A and B are joint together with a straight line, and uses interpolation to find the coordinate y_i of point C (which lies between A and B), assuming x_i (see Fig.6.1a). We used the fact that triangles ABE and CBD are similar when deriving the formula for y_i in terms of x_i.

Thus, since $(BE/AE) = (BD/CD)$, then $(y_2-y_1)/(x_2-x_1) = (y_2-y_i)/(x_2-x_i)$, from which y_i can be calculated for given values of x_i.

```
          1         2         3         4         5
 12345678901234567890123456789012345678901234567890
 C INTERPOLATION
         PRINT *,'ENTER VALUES FOR Y1 & X1'
         READ *,Y1,X1
         PRINT *,'ENTER VALUES FOR Y2 & X2'
         READ *,Y2,X2
    10   PRINT *,'ENTER VALUE FOR Xi BETWEEN X1 & X2'
         READ *,Xi
         IF (Xi .LT. X1 .OR. Xi .GT. X2) GOTO 10
         Yi=Y2-((Y2-Y1)*(X2-Xi))/(X2-X1)
         PRINT 20,Yi
    20   FORMAT(1X,'VALUE OF Yi IS EQUAL TO ',F10.2)
         STOP
         END
```

On execution, to test the program enter the coordinates for point A as 5.67 and 4.98 (for y_1 and x_1) and for point B the values of 9.21 and 11.32 (for y_2 and x_2).

──────────────── **Problem 6.1** ────────────────

Given the coordinates of two points A and B in the x-y system (see Fig. 6.1(b) above), write a program to calculate the equation of a straight line $(y = mx + c)$ joining the two points.

The program should read in the coordinates of the two points and calculate the slope $(m = BD/AD)$ of the line. It should then extrapolate the line to point $(0,y_e)$, thus working out the value of constant c. Finally the program should print out the equation of the straight line.

Use the fact that triangles ABD and EAF are similar when deriving the relation for y_e.

───

82

Integration – area under a curve

Integrating a function representing a curve between two specified limits in x, is identical to finding the area under a curve, between the same two limits (see Fig. 6.2).

(a) The trapezium rule

The easiest method to consider, at this stage, is the trapezium rule in which we assume that we can solve for the function at equal distances apart in x to obtain the vertical ordinates y_i. If we let this distance be d and we make it small enough, then the area under the curve between ordinates y_1 and y_2, say, can be approximated by the rectangle $\{y_1*d\}$, plus the area of the triangle at its top $\{(y_2-y_1)*d/2\}$, formed by drawing a straight line between the points where the ordinates y_1 and y_2 meet the curve. Thus the area under the curve between these two ordinates is equal to $\{y_1*d\} + \{(y_2-y_1)*d/2\} = d*(y_1/2 + y_2/2)$.

By similarly adding adjacent areas, due to y_3 etc, it can be shown that the area under a curve equals to

$$d * (y_1/2 + y_2 + y_3 + y_4 + \ldots + y_n/2)$$

where y_1 and y_n are the first and last ordinates, while d is the equal distance between ordinates.

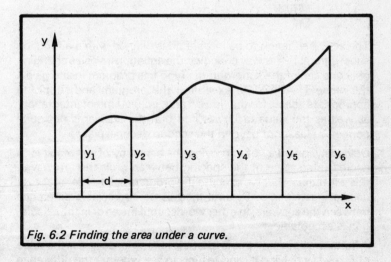

Fig. 6.2 Finding the area under a curve.

In the example below, we consider as a special case, the area under the curve $y = x^2$, calculated between $x = 0$ and $x = 10$. The width between ordinates is taken to be constant and equal to 0.2.

```
          1         2         3         4         5
12345678901234567890123456789012345678901234567890
C INTEGRATION BY THE TRAPEZIUM RULE
      REAL Lower, Last
      PRINT *,'ENTER LOWER LIMIT'
      READ *,Lower
      PRINT *,'ENTER UPPER LIMIT'
      READ *,Upper
      PRINT *,'STEP INTERVAL'
      READ *,D
      Area=D*Y(Lower)/2.0
      Area=Area+D*Y(Upper)/2.0
      First=Lower+D
      Last=Upper-D
      DO 100 X=First,Last,D
        Area=Area+D*Y(X)
 100  CONTINUE
      PRINT *,'AREA = ',Area
      STOP
      END
      FUNCTION Y(X)
      Y=X**2
      RETURN
      END
```

The actual equation to be integrated is defined within a function subprogram. In this way changing the equation involves changing only one line of the subprogram. Type this program in and give it the name TRAPEZ. On executing the program and supplying appropriate values for the 'lower' and 'upper' limit of integration, as well as the value of D, we find that the answer is not quite correct, at least not beyond the second decimal place.

Obviously, one way of improving the accuracy of the result is to decrease the value of the spacing between ordinates. However, this will require that we execute the program several times at ever decreasing values of D, until there is no appreciable difference between the answers; in other words, until the error in the calculation is acceptable.

A better way of doing this is to let the computer decrease the value of D, by say halving it, and testing to see whether the difference between the answers is less that an acceptable error.

84

Modify the TRAPEZ program so that the program assumes that the area under the curve is equal to zero, then calculates a new area with a value for D equal to half the difference between the upper and lower integration limits. If the difference between the two areas is less than, say, 0.0001 then D is halved and a newer area is calculated.

(b) Simpson's rule

A better approximation to the area under a curve can be obtained by the use of Simpson's rule which assumes that a polynomial can be fitted between the points where adjacent ordinates meet the curve, rather than a straight line.

Thus, if the area under a curve is divided into an even number of parts by an odd number of equidistant parallel ordinates y_i distance d apart, then the area under the curve is given by

$$A = d/3 (y_1 + 4y_2 + 2y_3 + 4y_4 + ... + 2y_{n-2} + 4y_{n-1} + y_n)$$

Note the way that ordinates are alternately multiplied by the two constants 4 and 2.

Iteration methods for finding roots of equations

(a) The Newton-Raphson method
The Newton-Raphson method states that, if x_i is the guessed root to the equation given by $F(x) = 0$, then a better approximation to the root, x_{i+1}, can be obtained by considering the following algorithm:

$$x_{i+1} = x_i - \frac{F(x_i)}{F'(x_i)}$$

where $F(x_i)$ is the original function, while $F'(x_i)$ is the value of the differential of the original function, both with x_i substituted into the expressions.

Referring to Fig. 6.3, suppose that R is the desired root of the equation $F(x) = 0$, shown plotted here; let x_0 be the initial approximation to the root (near enough to R) that the tangent cuts the axis at x_1. The point of intersection is then the second approximation. The process is repeated until the root is approached within a desired accuracy.

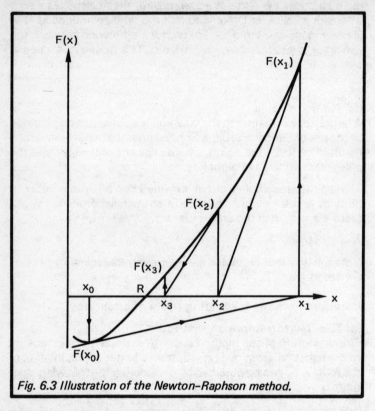

Fig. 6.3 Illustration of the Newton–Raphson method.

We can illustrate the technique by assuming we want to find the square root of 25. The original function and its differential can then be written as

$$F(x) = x^2 - 25 = 0$$

and

$$F'(x) = 2x.$$

Taking the guessed value to the root x_0 to be 1, we can substitute into the above two expressions for $x = 1$ to obtain

$$F(x) = (1)^2 - 25 = -24$$

and

$$F'(x) \, 2.(1) = 2$$

then substituting into the algorithm, we obtain a better approximation, as follows:

$$x_1 = 1 - (-24/2) = 13.000$$

Repeating the process, but now with $x = 13$, we obtain

$$F(x) = (13)^2 - 25 = 144$$

and

$$F'(x) = 2.(13) = 26$$

therefore,

$$x_2 = 13 - (144/26) = 7.462$$

Repeating again with $x = 7.462$, we obtain

$$F(x) = (7.47)^2 - 25 = 30.9$$

and

$$F'(x) = 2.(7.47) = 14.94$$

therefore,

$$x_3 = 7.47 - (30.9/14.94) = 5.406$$

Repeating once more with $x = 5.406$, we obtain

$$F(x) = (5.4)^2 - 25 = 4.16$$

and

$$F'(x) = 2.(5.4) = 10.8$$

therefore,

$$x_4 = 5.4 - (4.16/10.8) = 5.015.$$

Continuing in this manner, the approximation gets nearer and nearer to the desired value of 5.

Problem 6.3

Code the Newton-Raphson method (following the procedure given above) so that the square root of any number C can be found accurate to within four decimal places.

Write the program in the form of subroutine using a DO loop to limit the total number of iterations to, say 30, and arrange for a message to be printed out to signify non-divergence if that limit is exceeded. The main program should pass to the subroutine the number whose square root we want to find and the subroutine should pass back to the main program the final value of the answer to be printed out.

(b) The bisection method

This root-finding method does not involve differentiation, but requires that we have some idea where the root is to be found (see Fig. 6.4). We then solve for the function $f(x) = 0$ at two x points, one to the left of the root and the other to the right of the root, making a note of the sign of the remainder in both cases. We then take a point in x, midway between the 'left' and 'right' values of x and repeat the calculation, again making a note of the sign of the remainder.

In our illustration we see that the sign of the remainder in both the x_2 (the first midway point) and x_3 (the first 'right' point) positions is the same, therefore we make x_3 the new 'right' value for x. We then find a new midway point in x, between x_1 and x_3, to obtain a new remainder at point x_4 which then becomes the new 'left' x position as it has the same sign as x_1.

This process is repeated until the remainder of the function, obtained by substituting into the function the latest mid-point value x_n, is less than an acceptable error. An alternative (or additional) convergence test is an acceptable width interval between a final 'left' and 'right' points in x.

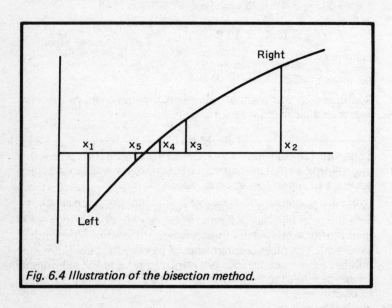

Fig. 6.4 Illustration of the bisection method.

The following program, which can find the square root of any number, illustrates the bisection method. The actual function is defined in a subroutine.

```
          1         2         3         4         5
12345678901234567890123456789012345678901234567890
C BISECTION METHOD FOR FINDING ROOTS
      REAL Left, Mid
      INTEGER Sign, Sleft, Sright, Smid
      PRINT *,'ENTER NUMBER TO FIND SQUARE ROOT'
      READ *,C
      Left=0.0
      Right=C
   10 Mid=(Right+Left)/2.0
      CALL BISECT(C,Left,Fleft,Sleft)
      CALL BISECT(C,Right,Fright,Sright)
      CALL BISECT(C,Mid,Fmid,Smid)
      IF (ABS(Left-Right) .LT. 0.001 .OR.
     & ABS(Fmid) .LT. 0.000001) THEN
         PRINT *,'SQUARE ROOT IS',Mid
         STOP
      ELSE
         IF (Sleft .EQ. Smid) Left=Mid
         IF (Sright .EQ. Smid) Right=Mid
      ENDIF
      PRINT *,Mid
      GOTO 10
      END
      SUBROUTINE BISECT(C,X,Fx,Sign)
      INTEGER Sign
      Fx=X**2-C
      Sign=1
      IF (Fx .LT. 0.0) Sign=-1
      RETURN
      END
```

On executing the program we see that the number of iteration required to reach a solution has increased by approximately three times compared to the Newton-Raphson method (compare the methods by finding the square root of, say, 36). However, the method can be used without having to differentiate a function, or indeed without having to have a function, as such, in the first place. This is illustrated in one of the exercises where the method can be used to calculate discounted cash flow.

(c) The secant method

In terms of convergence, the secant method (illustrated in Fig. 6.5) lies between the previous two methods, requiring more iterations than the Newton-Raphson but less than the bisection method. The method is illustrated graphically in Fig. 6.5. Given a function $F(x)$ and two points x_0 and x_1, we can find a new point x_2 by considering the two similar triangles in the illustration and writing

$$\frac{x_1 - x_2}{F(x_1) - 0} = \frac{x_0 - x_1}{F(x_0) - F(x_1)}$$

which, after rearrangement, can be written as

$$x_2 = x_1 - F(x_1) \frac{x_0 - x_1}{F(x_0) - F(x_1)}$$

Thus, given any two points and a function, we can find a third point which is closer to the required root without having to find the derivative of the function. By using iteration, this point can be made to approach the required root as closely as our converging criteria allow. One such converging criterion is that the absolute value of $x_0 - x_1$ is very small.

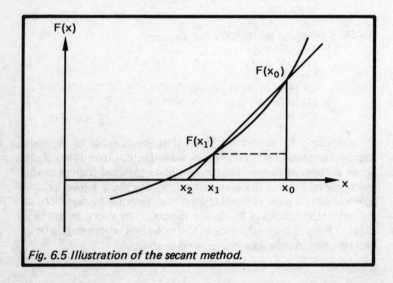

Fig. 6.5 Illustration of the secant method.

90

Solving simultaneous equations

There are a number of methods for solving simultaneous equations and exploring even a representative number of these is beyond the scope of this book. However, what we are interested in showing here is the algorithm building technique required in numerical methods. As such, we shall introduce two methods for solving simultaneous equations.

(a) The elimination method

The elimination method can be used to solve simultaneous equations. The program given below can solve two such equations for the two unknowns x_1 and x_2. The equations to be solved are:

$$3x_1 + 5x_2 = 6$$
$$5x_1 + 8x_2 = 12$$

The method can best be explained by first writing these equations in their general mathematical subscripted formulation which for the two simultaneous equations is as follows:

$$a_{11}x_1 + a_{12}x_2 = b_1$$
$$a_{21}x_1 + a_{22}x_2 = b_2$$

where a_{ij} and b_j are the coefficients of the equations.

Now, if the first equation is multiplied by $-a_{21}$ and the second by a_{11}, x_1 can be eliminated by addition, giving

$$x_2 = \frac{b_2 a_{11} - b_1 a_{21}}{a_{11}a_{22} - a_{12}a_{21}}$$

Similarly, by eliminating x_2, the value for x_1 can be obtained as

$$x_1 = \frac{b_1 a_{22} - b_2 a_{12}}{a_{11}a_{22} - a_{12}a_{21}}$$

The values of the coefficients a_{ij} of the equations are read into an array called A, while the values of b_i are read into an array called B. Consequently, the data must be supplied in the correct order, if the solutions are to be meaningful.

```
          1         2         3         4         5
123456789012345678901234567890123456789012345678901234567890
C SOLVING TWO SIMULTANEOUS EQUATION BY ELIMINATION
      DIMENSION A(2,2), B(2)
      DO 100 I=1,2
      READ *, (A(I,J), J=1,2)
  100 CONTINUE
      DO 200 I=1,2
      READ *, B(I)
  200 CONTINUE
C CALCULATE THE DENOMINATOR
      Denom=A(1,1)*A(2,2)-A(1,2)*A(2,1)
      IF (Denom .EQ. 0.0) THEN
        PRINT *, 'DENOMINATOR=0'
      ELSE
        X1=(B(1)*A(2,2)-B(2)*A(1,2))/Denom
        X2=(B(2)*A(1,1)-B(1)*A(2,1))/Denom
        PRINT *, X1, X2
      ENDIF
      STOP
      END
```

Thus, supplying the program with the correct data order as 3, 5, 5, 8, 6 and 12, results in the correct solution for x_1 and x_2 as 12.0 and -6.0, respectively.

However, the elimination method can become complicated once the number of unknowns, and hence the number of equations, are increased.

(b) The Gauss-Seidel method of iteration

The Gauss-Seidel method of iteration can be used to solve a large number of simultaneous equations, provided the main diagonal coefficient in each equation (i.e. a_{11}, a_{22}, a_{33}, ..., a_{nn}) is larger than all other coefficients in the equation.

Mathematically the equations can be expressed as

$$a_{11}x_1 + a_{12}x_2 + a_{13}x_3 = b_1$$
$$a_{21}x_1 + a_{22}x_2 + a_{23}x_3 = b_2$$
$$a_{31}x_1 + a_{32}x_2 + a_{33}x_3 = b_3$$

The method operates as follows:

(1) Guess the value of x_1, x_2 and x_3 (setting them to unity is good enough)

92

(2) Use x_2 and x_3 to solve the first equation for x_1, giving

$$x_{1(new)} = \frac{b_1 - a_{12}x_2 - a_{13}x_3}{a_{11}}$$

(3) Use $x_{1(new)}$ and x_3 to solve the second equation for x_2, giving

$$x_{2(new)} = \frac{b_2 - a_{21}x_{1(new)} - a_{23}x_3}{a_{22}}$$

(4) Use $x_{1(new)}$ and $x_{2(new)}$ to solve the third equation for x_3

If there are more equations, the same procedure is continued until all the equations have been solved and a new value for each unknown is obtained. This then constitutes one iteration. Further iterations are performed in a similar manner, always using the most recently calculated value of each x.

Tests for convergence, such as testing for the absolute value of $x_{new} - x_{old}$ being less than an acceptable small quantity for all values of x, must be included to stop the iteration. Further, a limit to the maximum number of iterations that can be performed must also be included.

The best way of writing this program is to incorporate a subroutine which solves for each new value of x, with a main program which is used to read in the values of a_{ij} and the values of the constants b_i, storing them in a two-dimensional array. The last column of the array should be reserved for storing the x values and that part of the array should be initialized to unity.

A DO loop should be used to control the number of iterations and the subroutine which solves for the new values of x_j should be called from within this DO loop. The values of x_j should then be returned to the main program for the convergence test, using as xold the values of x_j held in the array. If that test is not satisfied, the new value of x_j should then replace those in the array, and another iteration should start. This segment of the program is shown in some detail, while other parts of the program are only sketched in what follows.

Sketch of program using the Gauss-Seidel method

Dimension an array, say 50x50 to hold a_{ij} and b_j.

Read in N, the number of equations to be solved.

Use a DO loop to read the coefficients of N equations storing those of each equation in the first N columns of the array. Store the constants in the N + 1 column.

Initialize the N + 2 and N + 3 columns to unity to represent the x_{old} and x_{new} values, respectively.

Set up a DO loop to control the maximum number of iterations. Within this loop, first initialize a counter L to zero. This counter will be incremented later on by 1, each time the convergence test succeeds.

Set up a nested DO loop to call the subroutine, used to solve for x_j, N times. Each time program control is returned to the main program, test for convergence and increment L by one, if successful. If not, replace the contents of column N + 2 with those of column N + 3 in the array.

At the end of the nested DO loop test to see if L equals N. If it does, the solutions of all x_j have converged and the latest values, held in the N + 3 column of the array, can be printed out and the program stopped.

If L is not equal to N, allow program control to return to the beginning of the outer DO loop. This will re-zero counter L.

Try writing this program. You will learn a lot from the process. Use N = 3 and solve the following three equations.

$$3x_1 + x_2 + 2x_3 = 6$$
$$2x_1 + 3x_2 + x_3 = 1$$
$$x_1 + 2x_2 + 3x_3 = 5$$

If your program is written correctly, you should get the answers $x_1 = 1$, $x_2 = -1$ and $x_3 = 2$.

Having first used three equations in the subroutine in order to obtain solutions for the three unknowns, we now investigate a method whereby one generilized equation, referenced three times, can achieve the same result.

Note that when the subroutine is accessed with $I=1$ (for the first equation) $x_{1(new)}$, b_1 and a_{11} can easily be expressed in terms of I as x_I, b_I and a_{II}. This remains true for the other two equations when $I=2$ and $I=3$. The difficult terms to generalized are the product terms $a_{ij}x_j$ for each equation. However, on closer examination we can see that the missing products from each equation are those involving the diagonal a_{II} products.

For computational ease, we could re-write that part of the equation as the sum of the $a_{ij}x_j$ products and subtract from it the $a_{II}x_I$ product by writing

$$x_I = \frac{b_I - \Sigma(a_{IJ}x_J) + a_{II}x_I}{a_{II}}$$

thus reducing the three equations within the subroutine to one. The advantage of this algorithm is that it can be used to solve any number of simultaneous equations without having to change the program.

Note that I, above, refers to the control variable of the nested DO loop within the main program, the value of which must be passed to the subroutine through the argument list, while J refers to the control variable of a DO loop within the subroutine.

Assuming that the coefficients of the equations are stored in array A, the following schematic representation of the array can be drawn.

J $\longrightarrow$		N	N+1	N+2 x_{old}	N+3 x_{new}
I $\quad$ a_{11}	a_{12}	a_{13}	b_1	x_1	x_1
$\quad$ a_{21}	a_{22}	a_{23}	b_2	x_2	x_2
$\downarrow$ $\quad$ a_{31}	a_{32}	a_{33}	b_3	x_3	x_3

———————————— Problem 6.4 ————————————

With reference to the above layout of the contents of array A, write a subroutine to solve the general equation, as derived above. The sum of the products of $a_{ij}x_j$ can be calculated using a DO loop with control variable J.

Adjustable dimension arrays – The Parameter statement

The problem with the DIMENSION statement, as discussed so far, is that arrays were required to be dimensioned with actual numbers (we are not allow to use variables). In the particular problem examined previously, we suggested the use of 50x50 elements for the array A which had to be dimensioned in both the main program and the subroutine with the statement DIMENSION A(50,50). This would require changes to both the main program and the subroutine, should we later change our minds and want to increase the number of equations beyond the present size capability of array A.

One way of generalizing the program, is with the use of the PARAMETER statement which can be used to give a 'symbolic' name to a constant. This 'symbolic' name is not a variable and must be declared prior to the DIMENSION statement of the main program. Its value, which must not be changed during program execution, can then be passed to the subroutine via the argument list and used to dimension the array within the subroutine. For example,

```
      1         2         3         4         5
12345678901234567890123456789012345678901234567890
C MAIN PROGRAM TO SOLVE N SIMULTANEOUS EQUATIONS
      PARAMETER (N=3,Ncol=6)
      DIMENSION A(N,Ncol)
      .....
      .....

      CALL SOLVE(A,I,N,Ncol)
      .....
      .....

      STOP
      END
C SUBROUTINE TO SOLVE THE GENERAL EQUATION
      SUBROUTINE SOLVE(A,I,N,Ncol)
      DIMENSION A(N,Ncol)
      .....
      .....

      RETURN
      END
```

In this way, the size of the array is restricted to the minimum and is defined by the PARAMETER statement. The disadvantage is that the main program has to be recompiled each time the number of equations are changed.

96

An alternative solution, which avoids the need to recompile, is to dimension array A in the main program to its maximum capacity, say 50x50, but use a subroutine to read in the coefficients into an NxN+3 sub-section of it. This is important since subroutine SOLVE is expected to operate on the same sub-section of array A. Only by reading the coefficients of the given number of equations into a sub-section of array A, can we expect to find them in their correct placement later on when using subroutine SOLVE, which refers to the same sub-section of array A.

To achieve the above, we must change slightly the logic of the program. To this end, the main program is given below in full, while the subroutines appear in outline only.

```
          1         2         3         4         5
123456789012345678901234567890123456789012345678901234567890
C MAIN PROGRAM TO SET SIZE OF ARRAY A
      DIMENSION A(50,50)
      PRINT *, 'NUMBER OF EQUATIONS?'
      READ *, N
      Ncol=N+3
      CALL COEFIN(A,N,Ncol)
      PRINT *, 'NUMBER OF ITERATIONS?'
      READ *, K
      DO 100 Kount=1,K
        CALL SOLVE(A,N,Ncol)
  100 CONTINUE
      PRINT *, 'NUMBER OF MAX ITERATION EXEEDED'
      STOP
      END
C SUBROUTINE TO READ IN COEFFICIENTS OF EQUATIONS
      SUBROUTINE COEFIN(A,N,Ncol)
      DIMENSION A(N,Ncol)
      .....
      .....
      .....

      RETURN
      END
C SUBROUTINE TO SOLVE EQUATIONS & PRINT RESULTS
      SUBROUTINE SOLVE(A,N,Ncol)
      DIMENSION A(N,Ncol)
      L=0
      .....
      .....
      .....

      RETURN
      END
```

97

Exercises

1. Modify the interpolation program to use a subroutine. The main program should read in the coordinates of points A and B, and the x ordinates of point C, before passing the information to a subprogram through the argument list. The subprogram should return the value of y_i to the main program which should print the value of both x_i and y_i.

   The main program should be capable of calling the subprogram as many times as there are values of x_i for which the values of y_i are to be calculated.

2. Modify the solution to Problem 6.1 to incorporate a function subprogram. The main program should read in the coordinates of the two points and calculate the slope of the line. The function should be used to extrapolate the line to point $(0, y_e)$, thus returning the value of the constant c to the main program.

   Finally, the main program should print the actual equation of the straight line.

3. Modify the solution to Problem 6.2 so that Simpson's rule is used to find the area under a curve rather that the trapezium method.

4. Modify the solution to Problem 6.3 so that the Nth root of any number C can be found.

5. Use the Newton-Raphson method to calculate the roots of the equation

   $$0.1752\, r^3 - 2.2\, r^2 + 40.75 = 0$$

   where r is equal to the radius of a dragline base to be used on a local mining scheme.

6. Change SUBROUTINE BISECT in the Bisection program so as to use the SIGN function to find the sign of the Fx instead of the method used in the program.

7. The pattern of cash flow associated with a certain project can be represented by the diagram below. The construction of buildings and the installation of plant and machinery takes 3 years to complete (represented in the diagram by Years −2 to 0).

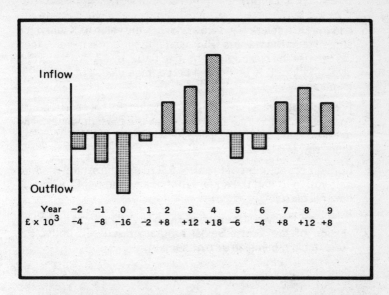

The project starts operating from Year 1, but because of additions to the capacity of the plant in that year, a net cash outflow is expected. The project starts to earn profits in Year 2, but a cyclic pattern is expected because of the price of raw material needed for the production of goods. This cyclic pattern gives sequences of positive and negative cash flows.

The first step in solving this problem is to relate the cash flows arising from the project to a common base year, namely, Year 0. Cash flows arising in years prior to Year 0 must be adjusted by an interest or earnings factor which must be added to the cost of the investment, in order to bring it to the correct value for the base year. Cash flows arising in years subsequent to Year 0 must be brought back to their value at the base year by means of discount factors that will reduce the value of the future receipts to their present values at the base year. The procedure is known as the Discounted Cash Flow (DCF) calculation.

Since the present value (PV) of an amount £C received after n years at X% interest rate, is given by

$$PV = \frac{C}{(1 + X/100)^n}$$

and the DCF solution we are seeking is the value of X when the sum of all present value (PV) cash flows is equal to zero, then we can use the bisection method to find X by taking as starting 'left' and 'right' X points the percentage values of 1 and 99, respectively.

For each value of X, find the present value (PV) of each C corresponding to each Year n, and sum all the present values. The required value of X is the value for which the ABS(ΣPV) is less than, say, 0.01.

8. Convert the solution of Problem 6.3 to use the secant method of iteration to find the square root of any number C within six decimal places.

9. Complete the two subroutines given in outline form in the last version of the Gauss-Seidel program discussed under the 'Adjustable dimension arrays' section.

7. FILING TECHNIQUES

Fortran distinguishes between internal and external files. An internal file is a character array or character variable, and as such it is a sequential file; that is, the file is a sequence of character array elements, each one of which is a record. The order of the record is the same as the order of the array elements. All records have the same length, that of the array elements.

Most Fortran files are external; that is, they are a physical device, or they are files which are known to the operating system. Such files are accessed, using the ACCESS = option, by two methods:

(a) by sequential file access, for files associated with 'sequential devices', such as the keyboard, screen, printer, and data files created in sequential form, and

(b) by direct file access, for random access files whose records can be read or written in any order.

Thus the two ACCESS = options are 'SEQUENTIAL' or 'DIRECT', with the default being 'SEQUENTIAL'.

Sequential files in data sorting

Many programming applications, such as manipulation of information on employees' records, require alphabetical sorting. To achieve this, we must draw on the technique developed earlier on (in Chapter 3) for sorting numbers, as well as on the program 'Three number sort' of the same chapter.

The technique we shall adopt is more or less the same as the one used previously except that string arrays are used rather than individual variables. This has the effect of reducing the required number of IF statements to one. The technique is illustrated below by applying it to the 'Employees' program which should have been stored under the filename EMPLOY. Additions to the program can be incorporated using your line editor on the source file of the EMPLOY program, saving the resultant program under the filename ALPHA. Your final program should now look as follows:

```
                1         2         3         4         5
       12345678901234567890123456789012345678901234567890
       C ALPHABETICAL SORTING
               CHARACTER*25 Employ(5),Temp
               OPEN(UNIT=3,FILE='EMPLOY.DAT')
               DO 100 I=1,5
                 READ (3,10) Employ(I)
         10      FORMAT(A25)
        100    CONTINUE
               CLOSE(UNIT=3)
               DO 200 I=1,5
                 PRINT *,Employ(I)
        200    CONTINUE
               PRINT *,'SORTED INFORMATION'
               DO 300 I=1,4
                 IF (Employ(I) .GT. Employ(I+1) THEN
                   Temp=Employ(I+1)
                   Employ(I+1)=Employ(I)
                   Employ(I)=Temp
                 ENDIF
        300    CONTINUE
               DO 400 I=1,5
                 PRINT *,Employ(I)
        400    CONTINUE
               END
```

Note that by omitting the ACCESS= option in the OPEN statement, Fortran takes the default value which is ACCESS='SE-
QUENTIAL' in accessing the external data file 'EMPLOY.DAT'.

On executing the program, the first five lines print the employees
in the same order as they appear in the data file. The second five
lines are the result of executing the DO-300 loop. Within this loop,
when I=1 the first string is compared with the second and if it is
found to be smaller, control is passed to the CONTINUE statement, otherwise the two strings are interchanged using Temp as a
temporary string for the swap. When I=2 the second string is
compared with the third, and so on until I=4, when the penultimate string is compared with the last. The result here is that
BROWN has moved one position up as follows:

```
WILSON M.  ,ROOM 1.24, 395
SMITH M.   ,ROOM 2.6 ,7315
JONES B.M.,ROOM 6.19,1698
SMITH A.A.,ROOM 2.12, 456
BROWN C.   ,ROOM 3.1 , 432
```

```
SORTED INFORMATION
SMITH M.    ,ROOM 2.6 ,7315
JONES B.M.,ROOM 6.19,1698
SMITH A.A.,ROOM 2.12, 456
BROWN C.    ,ROOM 3.1 , 432
WILSON M.  ,ROOM 1.24, 395
```

In order for BROWN to move to the top of the list we must repeat
the DO-300 loop N-1 times, were N is the total number of strings.
We shall do this by adding an extra DO loop, starting prior to the
DO 300 statement and ending after the 400 CONTINUE statement, as follows:

```
      DO 500 J=1,4
        DO 300 I=1,4
        ....
        ....
        ....
300     CONTINUE
      PRINT 20, J
 20   FORMAT(1X//,I2)
      DO 400 I=1,5
        ....
400   CONTINUE
      PAUSE 'Press <Return> to continue ...'
500   CONTINUE
      END
```

Add into your program the five additional lines; two to form the
DO-500 loop, two appearing between the 300 CONTINUE statement and the beginning of the DO-400 loop and one after the 400
CONTINUE statement. Re-compile and execute the program.
You will now see that information appears on the screen in such a
manner as to allow us to distinguish the result of each execution of
the outer DO loop (by the use of the PRINT 20 statement).

Scrolling of information on the screen is avoided by the use of the
PAUSE statement which temporarily suspends program execution until a blank line is entered (by pressing Return), when control
is returned to the program. The prompting string within the
PAUSE statement informs the user of the action required. Thus,
the results of each iteration of the J loop can be studied at leisure
before continuing with program execution. What you will see on
the screen is:

SORTED INFORMATION

```
1
SMITH M.   ,ROOM 2.6 ,7315
JONES B.M.,ROOM 6.19,1698
SMITH A.A.,ROOM 2.12, 456
BROWN C.   ,ROOM 3.1 , 432
WILSON M. ,ROOM 1.24, 395

Press <Return> to continue ...

2
JONES B.M.,ROOM 6.19,1698
SMITH A.A.,ROOM 2.12, 456
BROWN C.   ,ROOM 3.1 , 432
SMITH M.   ,ROOM 2.6 ,7315
WILSON M. ,ROOM 1.24, 395

Press <Return> to continue ...

3
JONES B.M.,ROOM 6.19,1698
BROWN C.   ,ROOM 3.1 , 432
SMITH A.A.,ROOM 2.12, 456
SMITH M.   ,ROOM 2.6 ,7315
WILSON M. ,ROOM 1.24, 395

Press <Return> to continue ...

4
BROWN C.   ,ROOM 3.1 , 432
JONES B.M.,ROOM 6.19,1698
SMITH A.A.,ROOM 2.12, 456
SMITH M.   ,ROOM 2.6 ,7315
WILSON M. ,ROOM 1.24, 395
```

Sending output to a sequential device

A sequential access must be used with all devices that do not allow explicit motion (other than reading or writing). The keyboard, screen, and printer are all 'sequential devices'. Thus, information can be sent from within a Fortran program directly to a parallel printer by including the statement

```
OPEN(UNIT=4,FILE='LPT1')
```

in the program prior to diversion of output.

This causes all subsequent information PRINTed from within the program to be sent to the printer. The statement

```
CLOSE(UNIT=4)
```

disconnects the printer.

The choice of unit number is the prerogative of the user. Had the specified FILE= been 'COM1' then output would have been diverted to a serial printer. The CLOSE statement must appear in a program after the statement which caused output to be sent to the specified device. Again, the omission of the ACCESS= option from within the OPEN statement, causes Fortran to take the default value which is ACCESS='SEQUENTIAL'.

The following program will PRINT the string XYZ on the printer.

```
            1         2         3         4         5
   12345678901234567890123456789012345678901234567890
   C PRINT OUTPUT ON PRINTER
          CHARACTER String*3,Q
          String='XYZ'
      10  PRINT *,'OUTPUT TO SCREEN OR PRINTER? (S/P)'
          READ 20,Q
      20  FORMAT(A)
          IF (Q .NE. 'S' .AND. Q .NE. 'P') GOTO 10
            IF (Q .EQ. 'P') THEN
              OPEN(UNIT=4,FILE='LPT1')
              WRITE(4,30) String
      30      FORMAT(1X,A)
              CLOSE(UNIT=4)
            ELSE
              PRINT 40, String
      40      FORMAT(1X,A)
            ENDIF
          END
```

─────────────────── **Problem 7.1** ───────────────────
Incorporate the above facility for printing the output of the ALPHA program either on the screen or on the printer.

Directing output to a file

Information can be sent from within a program to a sequential file by including the statement

```
OPEN(UNIT=4,FILE='SQFILE.DAT',STATUS='UNKNOWN')
```

in the program prior to writing to a file. Again, the choice of the unit number is left to the user. Once output has been written to the file, the file is CLOSEd. The following short program will serve to illustrate the point.

```
          1         2         3         4         5
12345678901234567890123456789012345678901234567890
C WRITING OUTPUT TO A SEQUENTIAL FILE
      CHARACTER String*3,Q
      String='XYZ'
10    PRINT *,'OUTPUT TO SCREEN OR FILE? (S/F)'
      READ 20,Q
20    FORMAT(A)
      IF (Q .NE. 'S' .AND. Q .NE. 'F') GOTO 10
        IF (Q .EQ. 'F') THEN
          OPEN(UNIT=4,FILE='SQFILE.DAT',
     &      STATUS='UNKNOWN')
          WRITE(4,30) String
30        FORMAT(A3)
          CLOSE(UNIT=4)
        ELSE
          PRINT 40, String
40        FORMAT(1X,A)
        ENDIF
      END
```

Use the TYPE command (at the DOS prompt, type the command TYPE SQFILE.DAT) to verify that indeed the file called SQFILE-.DAT contains the expected string.

Note the use of the STATUS = option in the OPEN statement. In this case we have used STATUS = 'UNKNOWN' because we were not certain that a file by the given name existed or not. There are other STATUS = commands, as explained below.

STATUS = 'OLD'   If 'OLD' is specified, the file must already exist. If the file does not exist, an error will be generated at execution. If an existing sequential 'OLD' file is opened and we write to it without first moving to the end of the file, the file is overwritten.

106

STATUS = 'NEW'	If 'NEW' is specified, the file must not exist already. If the file does not exist, a file is created, but if the file exists, then an error is generated at execution.
STATUS = 'UNKNOWN'	If 'UNKNOWN' is specified, the compiler first attempts to open the file with status equal to 'OLD', then with status equal to 'NEW'. This avoids execution errors.
STATUS = 'SCRATCH'	If 'SCRATCH' is specified with a named file, or no file name is specified when OPENing a file, a temporary scratch file is created. Scratch files are deleted at the end of program execution, or when closed.

The above STATUS = option is applicable to both sequential and direct files (the latter to be discussed shortly).

One record is written for each unformatted READ or WRITE statement, while a formatted READ or WRITE statement can transfer more than one record using the slash (/) control specifier. On output, incomplete formatted records are padded with spaces, while incomplete unformatted records are padded with undefined bytes. Formatted and unformatted records are declared with the FORM = option which can be either 'FORMATTED' or 'UNFORMATTED'.

In the case of sequential access files, the default value for the FORM = option is 'FORMATTED' (which is the reason why this option was not used within the OPEN statement in the examples used so far), while in the case of direct access files, the default value for the FORM = option is 'UNFORMATTED'.

――――――――――――――― Problem 7.2 ―――――――――――――――

Incorporate the above facility for writing the output of the ALPHA program either on the screen or to a file. Save the resultant program under the filename ALPHAWR.FOR in which name the letters WR stand for Write/Read.

Direct access files

Records in a random-access file are numbered sequentially, with the first record as number 1, and all records have the same length, specified by the RECL= option in the OPEN statement. Sequential data files, as we have used them up to now, can have different record lengths, and as such can occupy less space on disc. Records in a direct-access file can be read or written in any order by simply specifying the REC= option which indicates the record number to be read from or written to the file.

Attempting to read a record in direct-access mode, when that record was not written with the ACCESS='DIRECT' option within the OPEN statement, is illegal and can produce an execution error. If a record is written beyond the old file extend, the operating system attempts to extend the boundary of direct-access files, provided there is space on disc. It is not possible to delete a record once written; however, a record can be overwritten with a new value. The number of bytes written to a record must be less or equal to the record length.

The following program will help to illustrate some of the points raised above, as well as introduce some additional concepts.

```
          1         2         3         4         5
 12345678901234567890123456789012345678901234567890
C ALPHA SORT WITH OUTPUT TO RANDOM FILE
       CHARACTER*25 Employ(5),Temp
       OPEN(UNIT=3,FILE='EMPLOY.DAT')
       N=5
       DO 100 I=1,N
         READ (3,10) Employ(I)
  10     FORMAT(A25)
 100   CONTINUE
       CLOSE(UNIT=3)
       DO 300 J=1,N-1
         DO 200 I=1,N-1
           IF (Employ(I) .GT. Employ(I+1)) THEN
             Temp=Employ(I+1)
             Employ(I+1)=Employ(I)
             Employ(I)=Temp
           ENDIF
 200     CONTINUE
 300   CONTINUE
       OPEN(UNIT=4,ACCESS='DIRECT',FILE='RANSRT.DAT',
      &     FORM='FORMATTED',STATUS='UNKNOWN',RECL=25)
```

```
          DO 400 I=1,N
            WRITE(4,20,REC=I) Employ(I)
  20        FORMAT(A25)
 400      CONTINUE
          CLOSE(UNIT=4)
          OPEN(UNIT=3,ACCESS='DIRECT',FILE='RANSRT.DAT',
     &        FORM='FORMATTED',STATUS='UNKNOWN',RECL=25)
          DO 500 I=1,N
            Iback=N+1-i
            READ (3,30,REC=Iback) Employ(I)
  30        FORMAT(A25)
 500      CONTINUE
          CLOSE(UNIT=3)
          DO 600 I=1,N
            PRINT *, Employ(I)
 600      CONTINUE
          END
```

The program first reads the contents of the sequential file EMPLOY.DAT, sorts them alphabetically and then OPENs UNIT = 4 as a direct access file called RANSRT.DAT with a record length RECL = option of 25. In addition, the file is declared as 'FORMATTED' with the use of the FORM = option. This is necessary as we have used a FORMAT with the WRITE statement within the DO 400 loop, and the default of the FORM = option for a direct access file is 'UNFORMATTED'. Once the sorted records have been written to the file, UNIT = 4 is CLOSED.

Immediately following this, UNIT = 3 is assigned to the direct access file RANSRT.DAT and the DO 500 loop is set up to READ the records from the file. However, we choose to READ these records with the record number pointer set by REC = Iback. As the control variable I of the loop starts from 1 and is incremented by 1 until it reaches N, Iback is made to start from N and decrements to 1. In other words, the records in the file are read backwards into array Employ(I) which is subsequently printed out.

Thus, on execution the program reads the following five records

```
SMITH M.    ,ROOM 2.6 ,7315
JONES B.M. ,ROOM 6.19,1698
SMITH A.A.,ROOM 2.12, 456
WILSON M.  ,ROOM 1.24, 395
BROWN C.    ,ROOM 3.1 , 432
```

sorts them in alphabetical order and writes them into the file in the following order:

```
BROWN C.   ,ROOM 3.1 , 432
JONES B.M.,ROOM 6.19,1698
SMITH A.A.,ROOM 2.12, 456
SMITH M.   ,ROOM 2.6 ,7315
WILSON M. ,ROOM 1.24, 395
```

but subsequently these records are read from the file into array Employ() backwards, which when printed on the screen appear as

```
WILSON M. ,ROOM 1.24, 395
SMITH M.   ,ROOM 2.6 ,7315
SMITH A.A.,ROOM 2.12, 456
JONES B.M.,ROOM 6.19,1698
BROWN C.   ,ROOM 3.1 , 432
```

Error and end-of-file handling
If an error or end-of-file record is encountered during the execution of an I/O (input/output) statement, the action taken by the compiler depends on the presence of the ERR = , IOSTAT = and END = options. The PRINT statement does not allow any of these options to be specified. It will always produce an execution error.

The first two of these options (ERR = and IOSTAT =) are generally used within an OPEN statement to trap errors produced by the existence or otherwise of a file to be accessed. The action is as follows:

If, neither ERR = or IOSTAT = options a present	Then the program is terminated with an execution error
If, only ERR = label option is present	Then program control is transferred to the statement at 'label'
If, only IOSTAT = Icheck option is present	Then the value of 'Icheck' is set to a positive integer and program execution is continued
If, both ERR = label and IOSTAT = Icheck are present	Then the value of 'Icheck' is set to a positive integer and program control is transferred to 'label'.

110

The ERR= option can also be used in a READ statement to validate data input. For example,

```
          1         2         3         4         5
 12345678901234567890123456789012345678901234567890
 C VALIDATION OF INPUT
    10   PRINT *, 'ENTER AN INTEGER'
         READ (*,20,ERR=100) K
    20   FORMAT (I9)
         PRINT *, K
         STOP
   100   PRINT *, 'Invalid value. Please'
         GOTO 10
         END
```

The last option (END=) is generally used within the READ statement while accessing a file. If an end-of-file record is encountered while reading a file, an error is produced and execution stops, unless the END= option is used to divert execution to the label specified by the option.

The simple example given below (largely drawn from the previous program on sorting) will help to illustrate these points.

```
          1         2         3         4         5
 12345678901234567890123456789012345678901234567890
 C READING A SPECIFIED FILE WITH ERR=,
 C IOSTAT= & END= OPTIONS
         CHARACTER*25 Employ(5)
         CHARACTER Fname*6, Filename*10
    10   PRINT *, 'ENTER NAME OF FILE TO READ'
         READ (*,20) Fname
    20   FORMAT(A6)
         Filename=Fname(1:6)//'.DAT'
         OPEN(UNIT=3,FILE=Filename,STATUS='OLD',
        &ERR=400,IOSTAT=Icheck)
         PRINT *, 'HOW MANY RECORDS?'
         READ *, N
         Kount=0
         DO 100 I=1,N
           READ (3,30,END=200) Employ(I)
           Kount=Kount+1
    30     FORMAT(A25)
   100   CONTINUE
   200   CLOSE(UNIT=3)
         DO 300 I=1,Kount
           PRINT *, Employ(I)
   300   CONTINUE
         STOP
```

111

```
400   PRINT *, 'No such filename. Please'
      GOTO 10
      END
```

The purpose of the exercise is to allow a data file to be read. We need to specify only the name of the file without its extension, as the program adds this automatically. The file is also declared as 'OLD' in the STATUS = option within the OPEN statement as we certainly don't want to be creating empty files with the wrongly typed names. It is important that both the ERR = and IOSTAT = options are included in the OPEN statement to properly control program flow, as discussed earlier. If the specified file does not exist, then program control is diverted to statement 400, the ERR = label and the integer Icheck is given a positive value.

Following the OPEN statement, the program asks for the number N of records to be read. Unless the END = option is included in the READ statement, then the error resulting from encountering the end-of-file record (if N was larger than the total number of records in the file), would stop execution. Here this is avoided with the inclusion of the END = 200 option which diverts program control to statement 200 with variable Kount holding the total number of records in the file.

Save this program under the filename ROSFILE.FOR (for Read Old Sequential File), and compile it. On execution, supply the name of the sequential file SORTED (without the .DAT extension) and when asked for the number of records to be read, type any number greater than 5 (the actual number of records in the file). If you have reproduced the ROSFILE program correctly, then the five records of the data file SORTED will be read correctly and printed on the screen.

─────────────── **Problem 7.3** ───────────────
Incorporate data validation in the ROSFILE program so that no errors can occur by, say, responding with a non-integer entry to the question 'HOW MANY RECORDS?'.

Position of file READ/WRITE pointer

When a sequential file is OPENed, the file READ/WRITE pointer is positioned at the beginning of the file. If the next I/O operation is a WRITE, all old data in the file are lost as the pointer position after a sequential WRITE is at the end-of-file record. Thus, to append records to a sequential file we must first READ all the records in the file until the file READ/WRITE pointer is positioned after the end-of-file record. However, this produces an error, unless the END= option is included in the READ statement.

At this point we must execute the BACKSPACE statement in order to place the file pointer at the beginning of the end-of-file record, so that the next WRITE statement can be executed without causing overwriting of actual records. The following program will help to illustrate all of these points.

```
              1         2         3         4         5
     12345678901234567890123456789012345678901234567890
     C APPENDING RECORDS TO A SEQUENTIAL FILE
             CHARACTER*25 Employ(20),Temp(5)
             CHARACTER Fname*6, Filename*10
     10      PRINT *, 'APPEND TO WHICH FILE?'
             READ (*,20) Fname
     20      FORMAT(A6)
             Filename=Fname(1:6)//'.DAT'
             OPEN(UNIT=3,FILE=Filename,STATUS='OLD',
             &ERR=400,IOSTAT=Icheck)
     25      PRINT *, 'APPEND HOW MANY RECORDS? (1-5)'
             READ *, N
             IF (N .GT. 5) THEN
                PRINT *, 'LESS OR EQUAL TO 5 PLEASE'
                GOTO 25
             ENDIF
             DO 50 I=1,N
                READ(*,30) Temp(I)
     30      FORMAT(A25)
     50      CONTINUE
             Kount=0
             DO 100 I=1,20
                READ(3,30,END=200) Employ(I)
                Kount=Kount+1
     100     CONTINUE
     200     BACKSPACE 3
             DO 250 I=1,N
                WRITE(3,30) Temp(I)
     250     CONTINUE
             CLOSE(UNIT=3)
```

```
            OPEN(UNIT=3,FILE=Filename)
            New=Kount+N
            DO 280 I=1,New
              READ(3,30) Employ(I)
  280       CONTINUE
            CLOSE(UNIT=3)
            WRITE(*,40)
   40       FORMAT(//1X,'Records in file:')
            DO 300 I=1,New
              PRINT *, Employ(I)
  300       CONTINUE
            STOP
  400       PRINT *, 'No such filename. Please'
            GOTO 10
            END
```

The program, which we will call APPENDS (for Append to Sequential file), is an edited version of the ROSFILE program which was discussed previously. The APPENDS program allows us to append up to five records at a time to the existing records of a specified sequential data file.

Again, use the SORTED data file as the test file. Should you introduce any errors when typing the program, it is quite likely that on execution, the SORTED.DAT file will be corrupted. If that happens, re-execute the ALPHAWR program and send its output to a file (F) which will re-create the SORTED.DAT file.

The DO 50 loop accepts input from the keyboard and stores it in array Temp from which it will later be appended to the file. The DO 100 loop is used to find out how many records are already in the file (the result being stored in variable Kount) and to move the READ/WRITE pointer beyond the end-of-file record. Statement 200, BACKSPACEs the pointer to the beginning of the previous record (which is the end-of-file record) and the DO 250 loop causes information held in array Temp to be written to the end of the file (appended after the last record in the file). When all records have been appended, unit 3 is CLOSEd which writes and end-of-file record after the required additions. Finally, the file is re-OPENed in order to READ all its records (including the additions) and print them on the screen.

Exercises

1. Write a program to calculate the telephone charges for a given list of subscribers and print the results in a tabular form. The table must be sorted in order of subscribers' name and include the name, telephone number, units used and charge.

   The program should read in from a data file the names and telephone numbers into a subscripted string array and the units used into a numeric array in the order given in the data lines shown below. The telephone charges are to be calculated at 7 pence per unit.

Names	Phone No.	Units used
Smith A.J.	7141435	300
Jones M.M.	5743129	198
Adams N.P.	8466487	245
Brown J.G.	8673521	843

2. A record is kept of the production of each of the eight machines at a factory. At the end of each week, a data card is prepared for each machine with machine number (from 1 to 8), number of items produced and number of running hours. The information on these cards is then typed into a data file, not necessarily in order of machine number.

   Write a program to (a) calculate the number of items produced on each machine per hour, (b) add up the total production, (c) calculate the total hours worked, and (d) calculate the average production per hour. The results should be printed as a list in order of machine number under appropriate headings.

3. From the output of the ALPHA program you will notice two things:

   (a) After the first execution of the J loop, WILSON drops to the end of the list, and after every subsequent iteration the next highest valued name appears above WILSON.

(b) After each iteration of the J loop, BROWN moves up one position in the list of names.

This means that there is room for improving the program in two ways. Since the highest valued name drops to the bottom of the list, we can reduce the upper limit of the I loop by one for each execution of the J loop. Also, while the full N-1 iterations may be needed in the worst case, the list will often be sorted in somewhere between 0 and N-1 iterations. This can be overcome by incorporating a 'flag' in the program whose value is set to 0 normally, but is reset to 1 every time an exchange takes place. By testing for the value of the flag at the end of each iteration we can tell whether or not we need to execute the J loop once more.

Save the resulting program, under the filename BUBBLE.

4. Write a program which reads from a data file the names of several people into a subscripted string array and the telephone number extensions by which they can be contacted into a numerical array. The program should then sort and print the names in alphabetical order, keeping the connection between names and telephone numbers intact.

Format and use the following data to test the program.

Smith, A.J.	325	4747	555	
Johnson, B.	125	789	456	
Blackmore, S.	525	3567	625	
Adams, N.M.	111			
Brown G.E.	213	636		
Jones J.J.	989	5432	655	675
Williams D.	255			

5. Adapt the APPENDS program to append records to a direct access file. Use the RANSRT.DAT file as the test file. The file was created as a direct file and can be re-created by executing the RANDOM program which was discussed in the 'Direct access files' section.

8. APPENDIX A

The EDLIN line editor

MS-DOS provides you with a simple line editor, called EDLIN, and you should become familiar with its use. In general, EDLIN allows the creation and editing of ASCII files. These are text files which when sent to the screen or printer are interpreted as text.

EDLIN can also be used to create the source code of various programming languages, such as BASIC and Fortran. In such cases, remember to give the file the appropriate extension. For the two languages mentioned above, these will be .BAS and .FOR, respectively.

To invoke EDLIN, the MS-DOS System disc or a disc that contains it must be in one drive, and the file you want to create or edit must be specified. Thus, typing the command:

```
A>EDLIN TEST.TXT
```

expects to find both EDLIN and the fictitious file TEST.TXT on the disc in the logged drive (in this case A:), while typing

```
A>EDLIN B:TEST.TXT
```

expects to find EDLIN on the disc in the logged drive and the file TEST.TXT on the disc in the B: drive.

If the file does not exist on the specified disc, then EDLIN responds with

```
New File
*_
```

and waits for further commands, while if the file already exists, then EDLIN loads the file into RAM and responds with

```
End of input file
*_
```

Note the "*" prompt which is characteristic of EDLIN. Let us now create a text file, called TEST.TXT, which we will use to demonstrate the power of EDLIN. To start, type at the MS-DOS prompt

117

```
A>EDLIN TEST.TXT
```

which should cause EDLIN to respond with

```
New File
*_
```

if that file does not exist on your disc. If it does exist and you do not want to spoil its contents, then type q (for quit) and press the Return key.

The Insert command on a new file:
To insert lines of text, use the command i (for insert) at the prompt. In the case of a new file, as no lines of text exist in the file, type 1i and then type in the short text given below.

```
*1i
            1:*FIRST LINE OF TEXT
            2:*SECOND LINE OF TEXT
            3:*^C
*_
```

After typing 1i at the prompt, EDLIN responds by giving a new line number (in this case 1:) with an asterisk after it to indicate that this is the current line. At this point we type FIRST LINE OF TEXT. On pressing the Return key, EDLIN gives us an additional line number, now 2:*, into which we type SECOND LINE OF TEXT. Again, on pressing Return, we are offered a further line number, and so on. To end the insertion mode, type Ctrl C.

The List command:
To see what text is in the file, type l (for list) at the prompt, as follows:

```
*l
            1: FIRST LINE OF TEXT
            2:*SECOND LINE OF TEXT
*_
```

The line numbers are inserted by EDLIN so that you can refer to the line you want to edit. The * in line 2 indicates that this line was the last to be edited or inserted when EDLIN was used last. Note that now there is only one current line. Should the file you are listing be very long, listing in this manner causes the current line to appear in the middle of the listing.

118

To list specific lines, use the l command with line numbers. For example,

`*5,15l`

will list lines from 5 to 15 inclusive. Note the syntax of the command which is: "From line number to line number Command". There must be no comma between the second line number and the command letter.

The Edit mode:
To change the current line, type the new line number and press Return. This puts you in edit mode and will cause the line whose number you typed to be displayed. Pressing Return again, confirms that you are happy with the contents of that line, otherwise you can either press the right cursor key to reveal each letter of that line, or re-type the entire line, making any necessary changes. In our case, we want to change line 2 to

`SECOND LINE OF TEXT, EDITED`

so enter the edit mode and change the line appropriately. This is best done by using the right arrow cursor key to reveal the whole of the existing line and then typing the extra information at the end of it. The Ins and Del keys can also be used to edit the text.

The Insert command on an existing file:
To insert lines of text, use the command i (for insert) at the prompt. However, be warned. Using i by its own will insert the new line before the current line (the one with the * after the line number). To insert lines at any other point, give the line number before the command.

In our case, we would like to insert two additional lines after the existing two. To do this, type

```
*3i
           3:*THIRD LINE OF TEXT
           4:*FOURTH LINE OF TEXT
           5:*^C
*_
```

Again, insertion mode is terminated in line 5: by pressing Ctrl C. If we now list the contents of the file, we get:

```
*I
                 1:  FIRST LINE OF TEXT
                 2:  SECOND LINE OF TEXT, EDITED
                 3:  THIRD LINE OF TEXT
                 4:*FOURTH LINE OF TEXT
*_
```

Note that the last line to be inserted becomes the current line.

The Delete command:
To delete unwanted lines of text, use the d command (for delete) at the prompt. However, if you use the d command without any number associated with it, you will delete the current line (the one with the asterisk). Therefore, if you want to delete line 13, say, type

*13d

or if you want to delete a group of lines, type

*13,15d

which is translated as "lines 13 to 15 to be deleted".

The Move and Copy commands:
To move or copy text, use the m or c commands (for move or copy). These commands must be preceded by three numbers, as follows:

*13,15,8m

which is interpreted as "lines 13 to 15 to be moved to a position before line 8".

Similarly, the c command will copy a block and insert it before the given line. To move or copy a single line, the first two numbers in the command will have to be the same. After moving or copying lines, always use the list command to force renumbering of the file's contents.

The Search command:
To search for the occurrence of a word or a specified number of characters in a file you have created using EDLIN, use the search command. Just as in the list and delete commands, a line range is first specified, followed by the s (for search) command. Thus, typing

`*1,4s EDITED`

evokes the response

> `2: SECOND LINE OF TEXT, EDITED`
> `*_`

which displays the line containing the word EDITED.

Note that the space between the command s and the word EDITED becomes part of the search string. Had we been searching for the characters CON within the word SECOND, we would have had to omit the space between the command s and the string CON.

The search command finds only the first occurrence of the specified string. To continue the search for further occurrences of the same string, simply type s again. Thus, typing

`*1,4sIR`
> `1: FIRST LINE OF TEXT`

`*s`
> `3: THIRD LINE OF TEXT`

`*_`

causes EDLIN to first find the string IR in the word FIRST of line 1:, then by typing s again, it forces EDLIN to find the same string IR in the word THIRD of line 3:.

The Search and Replace command:
This command is similar to the search command, except that it requires a replacement string. Thus, typing

`*1,4r EDITED^Z RE-EDITED`

will cause *all* occurrences of the word EDITED to be replaced by the word RE-EDITED in *all* the specified lines of text. Here, of course, it only occurs once in line 2: of the text. The character ^Z is the two-key depression Ctrl Z (hold the key marked Ctrl down and press the Z key), which acts as a delimiter between the two strings.

Again note that the space in front of both words becomes part of both the searching and the replacing strings.

Exiting EDLIN:
To end the current session and exit EDLIN at any point, type

*e

which saves a new file under the chosen filename. However, if the filename already existed on disc prior to using EDLIN, ending EDLIN has the following effect: First the name of the old file on the disc is given the extension .BAK, then the new file you have created by editing the old one is saved with the original extension. In this way you can make mistakes without disastrous effects since the system makes a backup file of the original. If need be, you could DELete the .TXT file and then REName the backup file (.BAK) to its original name and extension.

Note that EDLIN is disciplined not to allow editing of backup files so, should you want to start using EDLIN to edit the contents of a .BAK file, you must first rename it, by giving it a different extension, before proceeding.

If, on the other hand, you realised that too many mistakes were made during editing, you could use the q command to quit, as follows:

*q

instead of using the e command as discussed above. Doing this causes EDLIN to ask you whether you want to abort. Typing Y (for yes), leaves the name and contents of the original file on disc unaltered.

If you intend to write complicated programs which might require extensive editing, then it is best to use a full screen editor or your word processor, provided your word processor can export files in ASCII format.

122

9. SOLUTIONS TO PROBLEMS

The numbers identifying the column position of program statements appearing at the top of each problem solution are not part of the source file and must not be typed into the editor.

Problem 1.1

```
          1         2         3
123456789012345678901234567890  --- column position

C TIME CONVERSION
      READ *, DAYS, HOURS, XMINS
      TOTMIN=DAYS*24.0*60.0+HOURS*60.0+XMINS
      PRINT *, 'TOTAL NUMBER OF MINUTES', TOTMIN
      STOP
      END
```

Note that the third variable in the READ statement (XMINS) is assumed to hold real values. That is why the variable name starts with X.

Problem 2.1

```
X1 = 10937
X2 = 98415
X3 = 7.5
X4 = 0.46875
X5 = 1175
X6 = 1200
X7 = 5.767636
X8 = 5.290026
X9 = 0.413333
```

Problem 2.2

```
            1         2         3         4         5
12345678901234567890123456789012345678901234567890
C INTEGRAL AND FRACTIONAL PARTS OF A NUMBER
      PRINT *, 'ENTER A VALUE'
      READ *, VALUE
      INTEG=VALUE
C INTEG HOLDS THE INTEGRAL PART OF VALUE
      X=INTEG
C X HOLDS A FLOATING POINT REPRESENTATION OF INTEG
      FRACT=VALUE-X
      PRINT 10
  10  FORMAT (1X,
      & 'ORIGINAL      INTEGRAL      FRACTIONAL')
      PRINT 20, VALUE, INTEG, FRACT
  20  FORMAT (1X, F8.2, I13, F15.2)
      STOP
      END
```

Problem 2.3

```
            1         2         3         4         5
12345678901234567890123456789012345678901234567890
C COST OF ELECTRICITY
      REAL LOWVAL
      PRINT *, 'ENTER LAST READING'
      READ *, LOWVAL
      PRINT *, 'CURRENT READING'
      READ *, HIVAL
C ASSIGN VALUES FOR `UNIT COST' & `FLAT RATE'
      UCOST=5.5
      FRATE=885
C CALCULATE TOTAL UNIT COST
      TUCOST=(HIVAL-LOWVAL)*UCOST
C CALCULATE OVERALL COST
      OVCOST=FRATE+TUCOST
      PRINT 10
  10  FORMAT (//5X,'TOTAL UNITS COST',6X,
      &'FLAT RATE COST',8X,'OVERALL COST')
      PRINT 20, TUCOST,FRATE,OVCOST
  20  FORMAT (1X,/3(10X,F10.2)/)
      STOP
      END
```

Problem 3.1

```
         1         2         3         4         5
12345678901234567890123456789012345678901234567890
C COMPOUND INTEREST
      INTEGER YEARS
      PRINT *,'ENTER ORIGINAL MONEY LENT'
      READ *,ORIG
      PRINT *,'ENTER INTEREST RATE'
      READ *,RATE
      PRINT *,'ENTER NO. OF YEARS'
      READ *,YEARS
      PRINT 10
10    FORMAT (3X,'YEAR',15X,'AMOUNT')
      DO 100 N=1,YEARS
        AMOUNT=ORIG*(1.0+RATE/100.0)**N
        PRINT 20,N,AMOUNT
20      FORMAT (1X,I5,10X,F10.2)
100   CONTINUE
      STOP
      END
```

Problem 3.2

```
         1         2         3         4         5
12345678901234567890123456789012345678901234567890
C THREE NUMBER SORT
5     PRINT *,'ENTER THREE NUMBERS'
      READ *,A,B,C
      IF (A .GE. 0.0) THEN
10      IF (A .LT. B .OR. B .LT. C) THEN
          IF (A .LT. B) THEN
            TEMP=A
            A=B
            B=TEMP
          END IF
          IF (B .LT. C) THEN
            TEMP=B
            B=C
            C=TEMP
          END IF
          GOTO 10
        END IF
        PRINT *,A,B,C
        GOTO 5
      END IF
      STOP
      END
```

125

Problem 3.3

```
             1         2         3         4         5
12345678901234567890123456789012345678901234567890
C  USE OF COMPUTED GOTO STATEMENT
       REAL LITRES,METRES,KILOS
       G=4.54609
       F=0.3048
       P=0.453592
       PRINT *, 'NUMBER PLEASE'
       READ *, VALUE
       PRINT *,'Gall-Lit/Feet-Metre/Pound-Kilo (1/2/3)'
       READ *, K
       GOTO (100,200,300),K
       STOP
  100  LITRES=G*VALUE
       PRINT *,VALUE,' GALLONS = ',LITRES,' LITRES'
       STOP
  200  METRES=F*VALUE
       PRINT *,VALUE,' FEET = ',METRES,' METRES'
       STOP
  300  KILOS=P*VALUE
       PRINT *,VALUE,' FEET = ',KILOS,' KILOS'
       STOP
       END
```

Problem 4.1

```
             1         2         3         4         5
12345678901234567890123456789012345678901234567890
C NEWTON'S METHOD OF FINDING SQUARE ROOTS
       PRINT *,'ENTER A NUMBER'
       READ *,Xvalue
       PRINT *,'GUESS A VALUE'
       READ *,Quess
       DO 100 I=1,30
         Ratio=Xvalue/Quess
         Aver=(Ratio+Quess)/2.0
         IF (ABS(Ratio-Quess).LT.0.001) THEN
           PRINT *,'SQUARE ROOT OF ',Xvalue,'=',Aver
           STOP
         ENDIF
         Quess=Aver
  100  CONTINUE
       PRINT *,'NOT CONVERGING IN 30 ITERATIONS'
       STOP
       END
```

126

Problem 4.2

```
          1         2         3         4         5
1234567890123456789012345678901234567890123456789 0
C TWO USER-DEFINED FUNCTIONS - VOLUME OF A CYLINDER
      PRINT *,'RADIUS OF CYLINDER?'
      READ *,Radius
      PRINT *,'HEIGHT OF CYLINDER?'
      READ *,Height
      Answer=Volume(Radius,Height)
      PRINT *,'VOLUME=',Answer
      PRINT *,'ROUNDED VOLUME=',Round(Answer,2)
      STOP
      END
      FUNCTION Volume(R,H)
      PI=3.141592654
      Base=PI*R**2
      Volume=Base*H
      RETURN
      END
      FUNCTION Round(Value,D)
      INTEGER D
      Round=AINT(Value*10**D+0.5)/10**D
      RETURN
      END
```

Problem 4.3

```
          1         2         3         4         5
1234567890123456789012345678901234567890123456789 0
C VOLUME OF CYLINDER - SUBROUTINE & FUNCTION
      EXTERNAL Round
      DATA PI/3.141592654/
      PRINT *,'RADIUS OF CYLINDER?'
      READ *,Radius
      PRINT *,'HEIGHT OF CYLINDER?'
      READ *, Height
      CALL Volume(Radius,Height,PI,Answer,Round,Rval)
      PRINT *,'VOLUME=',Answer,'ROUNDED VOLUME=',Rval
      STOP
      END
      SUBROUTINE Volume(R,H,PI,A,Subst,Rvalue)
      Base=PI*R**2
      A=Base*H
      Rvalue=Subst(A,2)
      RETURN
      END
      FUNCTION Round(Value,D)
      INTEGER D
      Round=AINT(Value*10**D+0.5)/10**D
      RETURN
      END
```

127

Problem 5.1

```
          1         2         3         4         5
12345678901234567890123456789012345678901234567890
C STOCKTAKING
      CHARACTER*16 Item(4), Name
      CHARACTER*8 Stock(4)
      OPEN(UNIT=5,FILE='STOCK.DAT')
      DO 100 I=1,4
        READ (5,10) Item(I),Stock(I)
  10    FORMAT(A16,1X,A8)
 100    CONTINUE
      CLOSE(UNIT=5)
  20  PRINT *,'WHICH ITEM?'
      READ 30, Name
  30  FORMAT(A16)
      IF (Name .NE. 'END') THEN
        DO 200 I=1,4
          IF (Item(I)(1:3) .EQ. Name) THEN
            PRINT *,Item(I),' >>>>>> ',Stock(I)(1:3),
     &        ' IN STOCK AT £',Stock(I)(5:8),' EACH'
          END IF
 200    CONTINUE
        GOTO 20
      END IF
      STOP
      END
```

Note: This program requires the following data file under the name STOCK.DAT in order to execute correctly.

```
          1         2         3         4         5
12345678901234567890123456789012345678901234567890
INK ERASER       200 0.10
PENCIL ERASER    320 0.15
TYPING ERASER    25  0.25
CORRECTION FLUID 150 0.50
```

128

Problem 5.2 (a)

```
          1         2         3         4         5
12345678901234567890123456789012345678901234567890
C PRINTING A LETTER BY SPECIFYING A NUMBER
      INTEGER POS
      CHARACTER ALPHA*26, LETTER
      DATA ALPHA/'ABCDEFGHIJKLMNOPQRSTUVWXYZ'/
      PRINT *,'ENTER LETTER POSITION'
  10  READ *,POS
      IF (POS .LT. 1 .OR. POS .GT. 26) THEN
        PRINT *,'PLEASE RE-ENTER'
        GOTO 10
      ENDIF
      LETTER=ALPHA(POS:POS)
      PRINT *,'THE REQUIRED LETTER IS ',LETTER
      STOP
      END
```

Problem 5.2 (b)

```
          1         2         3         4         5
12345678901234567890123456789012345678901234567890
C POSITION IN ALPHABET BY SPECIFYING A LETTER
      INTEGER POS
      CHARACTER ALPHA*26, LETTER
      DATA ALPHA/'ABCDEFGHIJKLMNOPQRSTUVXYZ'/
      PRINT *,'ENTER LETTER TO FIND ITS POSITION'
  10  READ 20, LETTER
  20  FORMAT(A)
      IF (LETTER .LT. 'A' .OR. LETTER .GT. 'Z') THEN
        PRINT *,'PLEASE RE-ENTER'
        GOTO 10
      ENDIF
      POS=1
      DO 100 I=1,26
        IF (LETTER .NE. ALPHA(I:I)) THEN
          POS=POS+1
        ELSE
          PRINT *,'IT IS IN POSITION No. ',POS
          STOP
        ENDIF
 100  CONTINUE
      END
```

Problem 5.3

```
          1         2         3         4         5
1234567890123456789012345678901234567890123456789 0
C STOCKTAKING
      CHARACTER*16 Item(4), Name
      DIMENSION Stock(4,2)
      OPEN(UNIT=5,FILE='STOCK.DAT')
      DO 100 I=1,4
        READ (5,10) Item(I),Stock(I,1),Stock(I,2)
  10    FORMAT(A16,F4.0,F5.2)
 100  CONTINUE
      CLOSE(UNIT=5)
  20  PRINT *,'WHICH ITEM?'
      READ 30, Name
  30  FORMAT(A16)
      IF (Name .NE. 'END') THEN
        DO 200 I=1,4
          IF (Item(I)(1:3) .EQ. Name) THEN
            PRINT 40,Item(I),Stock(I,1),Stock(I,2)
  40        FORMAT(1X,A16,' >>>>>> ',F4.0,
     &        ' IN STOCK AT £',F5.2,' EACH')
          END IF
 200    CONTINUE
        GOTO 20
      END IF
      STOP
      END
```

Note: This program requires the following data file under the name STOCK.DAT in order to execute correctly.

```
          1         2         3         4         5
1234567890123456789012345678901234567890123456789 0
INK ERASER        200 0.10
PENCIL ERASER     320 0.15
TYPING ERASER     25  0.25
CORRECTION FLUID 150 0.50
```

Problem 6.1

```
        1         2         3         4         5
1234567890123456789012345678901234567890123456789 0
C EXTRAPOLATION
        PRINT *,'ENTER VALUES FOR Y1 & X1'
        READ *,Y1,X1
        PRINT *,'ENTER VALUES FOR Y2 & X2'
        READ *,Y2,X2
        Slope=(Y2-Y1)/(X2-X1)
        Ye=Y1-Slope*X1
        PRINT 20,Slope,Ye
   20   FORMAT(1X,'EQUATION IS Y=',F6.2,'X+',F6.2)
        STOP
        END
```

Problem 6.2

```
        1         2         3         4         5
1234567890123456789012345678901234567890123456789 0
C INTEGRATION BY THE TRAPEZIUM RULE
        REAL Lower, Last
        PRINT *,'ENTER LOWER LIMIT'
        READ *,Lower
        PRINT *,'ENTER UPPER LIMIT'
        READ *,Upper
        PRINT *,'ENTER ACCURACY'
        READ *, Accur
        Area1=0.0
        D=(Upper-Lower)/2.0
   10   Area=D*Y(Lower)/2.0
        Area=Area+D*Y(Upper)/2.0
        First=Lower+D
        Last=Upper-D
        DO 100 X=First,Last,D
          Area=Area+D*Y(X)
  100   CONTINUE
        PRINT *,'AREA = ',Area
        IF (ABS(Area-Area1) .LT. Accur) THEN
          PRINT *,'VALUE OF D = ',D
        ELSE
          D=D/2.0
          Area1=Area
          GOTO 10
        ENDIF
        STOP
        END
        FUNCTION Y(X)
        Y=X**2
        RETURN
        END
```

131

Problem 6.3

```
          1         2         3         4         5
12345678901234567890123456789012345678901234567890
C NEWTON-RAPHSON METHOD OF FINDING ROOTS
      PRINT *,'ENTER NUMBER TO FIND SQUARE ROOT'
      READ *,C
      CALL NEWTON(C,1.0,Xnew)
      PRINT *,'SQUARE ROOT IS',Xnew
      STOP
      END
      SUBROUTINE NEWTON(C,Xold,Xnew)
      DO 100 I=1,30
        Fx=Xold**2-C
        Fxdiff=2.0*Xold
        Xnew=Xold-(Fx/Fxdiff)
        IF (ABS(Xnew-Xold) .LT. 0.00001) THEN
          RETURN
        ELSE
          Xold=Xnew
          PRINT *,'XOLD IS',Xold
        END IF
  100 CONTINUE
      PRINT *,'NOT CONVERGING IN 30 ITERATIONS'
      STOP
      END
```

Problem 6.4

```
          1         2         3         4         5
12345678901234567890123456789012345678901234567890
C SUBROUTINE FOR THE GENERAL GAUSS-SEIDEL EQUATION
      SUBROUTINE SOLVE(A,I,N,M)
      DIMENSION A(M,M)
      SUM=0.0
      DO 100 J=1,N
        SUM=SUM+A(I,J)*A(J,N+2)
  100 CONTINUE
      A(I,N+3)=(A(I,N+1)-SUM+A(I,I)*A(I,N+2))/A(I,I)
      RETURN
      END
```

Problem 7.1

Note that in this version of the program we have replaced the value of the upper limit of the control variables in all the DO loops by variable N or N-1, as appropriate, where N represents the total number of strings to be manipulated. N in this case is given the numeric value 5 in an assignment statement at the beginning of the program.

```
          1         2         3         4         5
12345678901234567890123456789012345678901234567890
C ALPHA SORT WITH OUTPUT TO SCREEN/PRINTER
      CHARACTER*25 Employ(5),Temp
      CHARACTER Q
      OPEN(UNIT=3,FILE='EMPLOY.DAT')
      N=5
      DO 100 I=1,N
        READ (3,10) Employ(I)
 10     FORMAT(A25)
100   CONTINUE
      CLOSE(UNIT=3)
 50   PRINT *,'OUTPUT TO SCREEN OR PRINTER? (S/P)'
      READ 60,Q
 60   FORMAT(A)
      IF (Q .NE. 'S' .AND. Q .NE. 'P') GOTO 50
      IF (Q .EQ. 'P') THEN
        OPEN(UNIT=4,FILE='LPT1')
      ENDIF
      DO 200 I=1,N
        IF (Q .EQ. 'P') THEN
          WRITE(4,70) Employ(I)
 70       FORMAT(1X,A)
        ELSE
          PRINT *,Employ(I)
        ENDIF
200   CONTINUE
      IF (Q .EQ. 'P') THEN
        WRITE(4,20)
      ELSE
        PRINT 20
 20     FORMAT(1X/,' SORTED INFORMATION')
      ENDIF
      DO 500 J=1,N-1
        DO 300 I=1,N-1
          IF (Employ(I) .GT. Employ(I+1)) THEN
            Temp=Employ(I+1)
            Employ(I+1)=Employ(I)
            Employ(I)=Temp
          ENDIF
```

```
300    CONTINUE
       IF (Q .EQ. 'P') THEN
          WRITE(4,30) J
       ELSE
          PRINT 30, J
 30       FORMAT(1X/,I2)
       ENDIF
       DO 400 I=1,N
          IF (Q .EQ. 'P') THEN
             WRITE(4,80) Employ(I)
 80          FORMAT(1X,A)
          ELSE
             PRINT *,Employ(I)
          ENDIF
400    CONTINUE
       IF (Q .EQ. 'P') THEN
          WRITE(4,90)
 90       FORMAT(1X//)
          CLOSE(UNIT=4)
       ELSE
          PRINT *,' '
       ENDIF
       STOP
       IF (Q .EQ. 'S') THEN
          PRINT *,' '
          PAUSE 'Press <Return> to continue ...'
       ENDIF
500    CONTINUE
       END
```

Problem 7.2

```
          1         2         3         4         5
12345678901234567890123456789012345678901234567890
C ALPHA SORT WITH OUTPUT TO SCREEN/FILE
      CHARACTER*25 Employ(5),Temp
      CHARACTER Q
      OPEN(UNIT=3,FILE='EMPLOY.DAT')
      N=5
      DO 100 I=1,N
        READ (3,10) Employ(I)
 10     FORMAT(A25)
100   CONTINUE
      CLOSE(UNIT=3)
 20   PRINT *,'OUTPUT TO SCREEN OR FILE? (S/F)'
      READ 30,Q
 30   FORMAT(A)
      IF (Q .NE. 'S' .AND. Q .NE. 'F') GOTO 20
      IF (Q .EQ. 'S') THEN
        DO 200 I=1,N
          PRINT *,Employ(I)
200     CONTINUE
        PRINT 40
 40     FORMAT(1X/,' SORTED INFORMATION')
      ENDIF
      DO 500 J=1,N-1
        DO 300 I=1,N-1
          IF (Employ(I) .GT. Employ(I+1)) THEN
            Temp=Employ(I+1)
            Employ(I+1)=Employ(I)
            Employ(I)=Temp
          ENDIF
300     CONTINUE
        IF (Q .EQ. 'S') THEN
          PRINT 50, J
 50       FORMAT(1X/,I2)
          DO 400 I=1,N
            PRINT *,Employ(I)
400       CONTINUE
          PRINT *,' '
          PAUSE 'Press <Return> to continue ...'
        ENDIF
500   CONTINUE
      IF (Q .EQ. 'F') THEN
        OPEN(UNIT=4,FILE='SORTED.DAT',
     &       STATUS='UNKNOWN')
        DO 600 I=1,N
          WRITE(4,60) Employ(I)
 60       FORMAT(A25)
600     CONTINUE
```

135

```
        CLOSE(UNIT=4)
        OPEN(UNIT=3,FILE='SORTED.DAT')
        DO 700 I=1,N
          READ (3,70) Employ(I)
70        FORMAT(A25)
700     CONTINUE
        CLOSE(UNIT=3)
        DO 800 I=1,N
          PRINT *, Employ(I)
800     CONTINUE
      ENDIF
      END
```

Problem 7.3

```
            1         2         3         4         5
   12345678901234567890123456789012345678901234567890
C READING A SPECIFIED FILE WITH ERR=,
C IOSTAT= & END= OPTIONS
C INCLUDING INPUT DATA VALIDATION
        CHARACTER*25 Employ(5)
        CHARACTER Fname*6, Filename*10
   10   PRINT *, 'ENTER NAME OF FILE TO READ'
        READ (*,20) Fname
   20   FORMAT(A6)
        Filename=Fname(1:6)//'.DAT'
        OPEN(UNIT=3,FILE=Filename,STATUS='OLD',
       &ERR=400,IOSTAT=Icheck)
   22   PRINT *, 'HOW MANY RECORDS?'
        READ (*,25,ERR=500) N
   25   FORMAT(I1)
        Kount=0
        DO 100 I=1,N
          READ (3,30,END=200) Employ(I)
          Kount=Kount+1
   30     FORMAT(A25)
  100   CONTINUE
  200   CLOSE(UNIT=3)
        DO 300 I=1,Kount
          PRINT *, Employ(I)
  300   CONTINUE
        STOP
  400   PRINT *, 'No such filename. Please'
        GOTO 10
  500   PRINT *, 'Invalid value. Please re-enter'
        GOTO 22
        END
```

136

INDEX

137

Notes

Notes

Notes

Notes

PLEASE NOTE

Please note following is a list of other titles that are available in our range of Radio, Electronics and Computer books.

These should be available from all good Booksellers, Radio Component Dealers and Mail Order Companies.

However, should you experience difficulty in obtaining any title in your area, then please write directly to the publisher enclosing payment to cover the cost of the book plus adequate postage.

If you would like a complete catalogue of our entire range of Radio, Electronics and Computer Books then please send a Stamped Addressed Envelope to:

BERNARD BABANI (publishing) LTD
THE GRAMPIANS
SHEPHERDS BUSH ROAD
LONDON W6 7NF
ENGLAND